Hydroponics for the Home Gardener

Hydroponics for the Home Gardener

Stewart Kenyon

Foreword by Howard M. Resh

Van Nostrand Reinhold Ltd., *Toronto*
New York, Cincinnati, London, Melbourne

Library of Congress Catalogue Number 79-66492

Canadian Cataloguing in Publication Data

Kenyon, Stewart, 1932 –
    Hydroponics for the home gardener

Bibliography: p.
Includes index.
ISBN 0-442-29702-5

1. Hydroponics, I. Title.

SB126.5.K35   631.5'85   C79-094699-8

Editorial Consultant: James Wills
Design: Julian Cleva
Illustrations and cover: Doug Martin
Typesetting: Fleet Typographers Limited
Printing and binding: R.R. Donnelley & Sons Company
Printed and bound in the United States of America

79 80 81 82 83 84 85   7 6 5 4 3 2 1

To my mother, who would have enjoyed this book.

Contents

Foreword

Only five years ago the term hydroponics was little known by the majority of people. Even though it was being practiced by many commercial growers of vegetables and flowers earlier than that time, it was not commonly understood or used by the backyard or apartment garden enthusiast.

Today, almost every person has become aware of the potential of hydroponics, both commercially and around the home. Over the past three to four years, many books have been written on hydroponics, but the majority have been aimed at the backyard greenhouse gardener, while a few have been written for the commercial grower. Very few have been dedicated to the apartment or indoor gardener.

Hydroponics for the Home Gardener is the first book that I am aware of that fills this gap by thoroughly discussing the use of hydroponics for the small-scale indoor grower. As Mr. Kenyon points out in his introduction, this is a methods book. It is not an exhaustive scientific review, but rather a guide that describes how to make hydroponics work for you at home. The roles of light, temperature and nutrition are discussed in terms that are understandable by the layman. I am particularly pleased with his explanation of the similarities between organic gardening and hydroponics. The author gives us a number of easy-to-follow nutrient formulations and describes which fertilizers and the amounts of each to use. In addition, possible nutritional disorders are outlined along with easy methods to use in correcting them. A brief and clear explanation of pH, how to measure and adjust it, and a list of plants and their optimum pH ranges are given in Chapter 4.

Chapters 6 to 8 explore methods of growing vegetables and herbs hydroponically. All the basic information on varieties, nutrients, temperature and medium best suited for the indoor growing of these plants is outlined. I found one of the most interesting parts of the book to be the description not only of growing herbs but also their use in various recipes.

Hydroponics for the Home Gardener is concerned with results, and it goes on to detail how to obtain the highest yields from your soilless garden by extending the growing season outside, intercropping and outcropping on your balcony. Pollination, insect control, trouble shooting and control measures for various vegetables are all reviewed.

Overall, *Hydroponics for the Home Gardener* thoroughly discusses the basics of hydroponics for the beginner, with the indoor gardener always in mind. If the methods, plant needs and care described in the text are followed, anyone can grow plants sucessfully hydroponically. This is a very useful book for the person who has heard about hydroponics and wishes to begin growing plants in a very inexpensive system.

Once you read this book and try a few experiments, your success will inspire you to further research into the subject, and you will probably want to expand your hydroponic garden by building more trays, or perhaps, if you have the space, you may wish to purchase or build your own backyard hydroponic greenhouse. I know many people who have done just that. They started with a small indoor unit, were encouraged by their success, and within a year were growing fresh herbs, lettuce, tomatoes, cucumbers and other vegetables year-round in a fully climate-controlled hydroponic greenhouse.

As Mr. Kenyon points out, hydroponics depends to a large extent on experimentation and innovation. *Hydroponics for the Home Gardener* is the first book to give you the basics in a thorough and understandable way. After you have used this book to guide you to productive home hydroponics, it is up to you to experiment on your own and to share the results of this exciting new hobby.

Howard M. Resh, Ph.D.

Preface

I became involved in the field of home hydroponic gardening for several reasons. The freshness and flavour of the vegetables and herbs and their high nutritional value impressed me. After tasting a hydroponically grown vegetable, it was impossible to go back to the wilted, store-bought variety. I liked the fact that you could grow several crops of vegetables each year at a fraction of their supermarket cost. I knew many people who didn't have the time or space for a soil garden and who would welcome a method of growing plants that was easy and possible to do indoors or outdoors, in the living room or on an apartment balcony. And perhaps most importantly, here was a growing system that was environmentally sound, because it recycled water and nutrients until they had been used by the plants.

Hydroponics is one way that each of us can contribute to the quality of our environment. Imagine the amount of energy that is used to move fresh vegetables from Mexico, Jamaica or California to con-sumers in Canada or the northern United States. Using hydroponics, you can easily have your own environmentally sound vegetable garden in the kitchen, living room or basement.

Two things prompted me to write *Hydroponics for the Home Gardener*. There are many experts around the world in the field of hydroponics. In the past, they have primarily been involved in the areas of commercial growing or scientific research, and it is difficult for the amateur to relate to them and vice-versa. This book is an attempt to bridge that gap. It was written in response to the need to provide all the information necessary to get a respectable crop the first time, while leaving it up to the home grower to decide how deeply involved he wants to become in the more technical side of things. In our store, we have sold as many as six books on hydroponics, each of which has a great deal to say about commercial and greenhouse growing. This means that the books have relatively limited value for the home gardener. To my mind, the beginner desperately needed one book that would get him or her started and guided through the first crucial crop. I sincerely hope that this book fills that need.

Hydroponics for me, as it will be for you, is a continuous learning experience, and as time goes on I will gather more information that I would like to share with you. For this reason, I would welcome your letters if you feel that you can enhance our knowledge collectively, or if you are unable to find answers to your questions. I do not pretend to have all the answers now, nor am I an expert in the scientific sense, but I am committed to home hydroponics.

I have had a lot of help from many people. Special recognition must go to Helmut Julinot, a man who truly thinks in global terms. He is able to translate thought into action with incredible energy, and in his way he is contributing to the solutions of world problems. It was Helmut who helped me bridge the gap between theoretical and practical hydroponics, and it is his many friends at Starseed Farms that help prove every day that his ideas work.

Indirect help came from previously published books, which are listed in the bibliography. Of these I would particularly like to mention the excellent book by Howard Resh, *Hydroponic Food Production.*

Recognition would not be complete if I failed to thank Stuart Robertson of Applied Hydroponics of Canada for his help and suggestions on lighting, and Jim Wills and Laurie Coulter, the editors at Van Nostrand Reinhold Ltd., who deserve great praise for the weeks of time they have spent in helping me put it all together. Of course, none of this would have happened if Garry Lovatt, Vice-President at Van Nostrand Reinhold Ltd., had not supported me. The world is replete with authors without publishers, and I owe Garry a special debt of gratitude.

The unsung heroes who dared to try something different should also be mentioned. Early pioneers like Gericke and Douglas, more recent researchers and commercial growers, and the home growers around the world, all deserve praise.

And finally, I would like to extend particular thanks to my brother, Walter, and my wife, Sharon, for being my best supporters and for their help and encouragement.

S.K.
City Green Hydroponics Inc.
1134 Yonge Street
Toronto, Ontario, Canada
July 17, 1979

Hydroponics for the Home Gardener

CHAPTER 1

An Introduction to Hydroponics

*Hy'dro pŏn'ics: The art of cultivating plant life in a
nutrient-water solution whose roots are supported by a substance
other than soil.*

This could be considered a fairly accurate definition of the term
"hydroponics." In its more advanced stages, hydroponics can be a
complex art indeed, but the purpose of this book is to describe a series of
methods that will make hydroponics work for you. It will describe how
to make or where to buy a hydroponic system, how to plant it, how to
maintain it, how to correct common problems, and where to get
supplies. Two of the greatest benefits of hydroponic gardening are the
freshness and high nutritional value of the vegetables and herbs that
can be grown. For these reasons, you will also find recipes from famous
chefs who use hydroponically grown produce in their own kitchens.

What this book will not do is give a lengthy history of the subject,
or a great many personal anecdotes that do little good in helping you get
results from hydroponics. Presumably, results are the reason you bought
this book. By following the procedures listed here you will be able, for
example, to raise several crops of garden vegetables per year at a fraction
of their supermarket cost.

With the exception of a cursory knowledge of how hydroponics came about, most readers could care less about the long list of people who have experimented with hydroponics, or when. Nor do most readers care that some nutrients can be "locked in" under certain conditions and are therefore unavailable to the plant. These things can be found in the books listed in the bibliography. Here we will be dealing with only some of the hundreds of formulae where all the nutrients are available to the plant. In other words, I will not be giving you a lot of superfluous scientific information. If anyone feels that I haven't given enough background or scientific information, then they'll have to consult other books, because *Hydroponics for the Home Gardener* is written expressly to give you the facts you need.

History

Hydroponics is at least as ancient as the Pyramids. The Hanging Gardens of Babylon, which are listed as one of the Seven Wonders of the World, used a crude form of hydroponics. The world's rice crops have been grown in this way from time immemorial. In 1934, however, a University of California professor adapted this time-tested technique to other crops. The results were twenty-five foot tomato vines that had to be harvested with ladders. Modern hydroponics was born and it has been advancing ever since.

During the Second World War, Allied soldiers ate hydroponic vegetables grown on their air and naval bases in the South Pacific. Today, hydroponic installations help feed millions of people; they may be found flourishing in the deserts of Israel, Lebanon and Kuwait, on the islands of Ceylon, the Phillipines and the Canaries, on the roof tops of Calcutta and in the parched villages of West Bengal.

Half of Vancouver Island's tomato crop and one-fifth of Moscow's are hydroponically produced. There are full-fledged hydroponic systems in American nuclear submarines, Russian space stations and on off-shore drillings rigs. Large zoos keep their animals healthy with hydroponic green food, and race horses stay sleek and powerful on grass grown hydroponically year round. There are large and small systems used by companies and individuals as far north as Baffin Island and Eskimo Point in Canada's Arctic. Commercial growers are using this marvellous technique to produce food on a large scale from Israel to India, and from Armenia to the Sahara.

Is It Worthwhile?

Gardeners love hydroponics, because almost anything can be grown and there is no back-breaking work: no tilling, raking or hoeing. There are no weeds to pull, no poisonous pesticides to spray. No moles or cutworms eat your roots, and most insects leave your clean and healthy plants alone.

Hydroponics is ideal for the hobbyist home-owner or apartment-dweller who doesn't have the time or space for full-time soil gardening. In late spring and summer, your portable hydroponic unit can be put outside on a porch or balcony where natural sunlight helps produce tremendous yields of anything from lettuce, to cucumbers, to zinnias. In winter, the unit can be moved anywhere inside the home, even into the basement, where your plants will flourish and continue to produce under artificial light.

Plants love to grow in hydroponics, because their roots don't have to push through heavy, chunky soil to compete for nutrients. Instead, a hydroponic system distributes nutrients evenly to each plant. What's more, plants need air to breathe, and, unlike soil, a porous growing aggregate lets air circulate freely around them. Consequently, everything grows quickly and beautifully.

Hydroponic plants grow faster, ripen earlier and give up to ten times the yield of soil-grown plants. These clean and pampered plants produce fruits and vegetables of great nutritive value and superior flavour. Many of them, especially hydroponic tomatoes and cucumbers, are sold in the gourmet sections of supermarkets at considerably higher prices than ordinary vegetables. The point here is that you can grow the same vegetables for considerably *less* money than it costs to buy the pulpy supermarket variety.

Why Hydroponics For You?

Have you noticed lately that there's something missing in supermarket vegetables? It's flavour. As in many modern foods, flavour has been traded for the convenience of the producers. Large-scale farming and marketing do, of course, provide vast quantities of food for the world's burgeoning population, but it is important to remember that whenever quantity is stressed, quality suffers. Consequently, the flavour and nutritional value of your meals are reduced.

One major reason for these losses is the types of seeds developed for "agribusiness." These seeds are chosen for fast growth and high yields. The vegetables and fruits that result have tough skins for machine harvesting, sorting and shipping. Flavour and quality are secondary concerns. In addition, many vegetables – especially tomatoes – are harvested unripe to ensure safe shipment and a longer shelf life in the store. In fact, attempts are now being made to develop a hybrid, package-fitting square tomato.

In pioneer days, more often than not, towns and villages grew up where farmers tilled the soil. They were good farmers and chose the best soil. These towns and villages are our cities of today; still expanding, still gobbling up valuable farming land. As prime agricultural land disappears, as growers' costs keep rising, as transportation costs increase on a parallel with energy supplies and as supermarket boards of directors become more and more concerned with profit margins, we are going to see our food costs increase to the point of absurdity. The Victory Gardens of World War II were planted to raise unavailable food, and it seems realistic to say that in the near future millions of people will be using hydroponics to supply themselves with affordable vegetables and herbs of a quality that stores will not be able to match.

How Plants Grow

Some books on hydroponics give the reader a crash course on biology complete with diagrams. I would prefer that you get your own biology text, if you feel it's necessary in order to produce good cucumbers. It seems to make more sense to relate biology directly to hydroponics and the nutrients that make plants grow.

Each plant is a natural workshop that builds organic matter in the form of roots, stems, leaves, fruit and seeds. Air and water provide more than ninety-seven per cent of this matter, while the remainder comes from plant nutrients. A plant cannot take up any organic substance; rather it absorbs inorganic mineral salts. That is, the vegetable kingdom feeds directly on the mineral kingdom.

This is why there is no conflict between organic gardening and hydroponics. The difference is, however, that in organic gardening it is the soil that is fed with dead plant and animal matter, not the plant. Soil acts as a natural fertilizer factory that goes to work on these organic substances with its soil bacteria in league with weathering. It breaks these substances down into their inorganic parts (chemicals, if you like), so that the plants can feed on them.

In hydroponics there is no soil, and the plants are fed directly with the same minerals that healthy organic soil produces. The plant does not know, or particularly care, whether its mineral food was made by man or nature. It does care, though, that it is well fed, and a nitrate is a nitrate whether it comes from a nutrient solution or a dead mouse.

A plant uses two basic processes in order to grow. The first, osmosis, takes up water and minerals through the roots. The second, photosynthesis, uses light and the atmosphere for transforming the water and minerals into plant tissue. Roots need air as well, in order to breathe, and this is one of the reasons that hydroponics works so well. The loose, chunky hydroponic growing medium, the aggregate, as it is called, allows plenty of air to reach the roots. On the other hand, natural soil often requires a lot of work and time to assure satisfactory aeration.

AGGREGATE

NUTRIENT SOLUTION

Figure 1. A simple hydroponic system.

Chemicals or No Chemicals?

Are chemicals used in hydroponics? Most people would say no, but the real answer is yes. We will be using a mixture of N_2 and O_2, commonly called air, and lots of H_2O. To this is added small amounts of N, P and K (nitrogen, phosphorous and potassium) and balanced trace elements. The serious point being made here is that the world and everything in it is made up of one "chemical" or another. What we do avoid in hydroponics is putting the wrong chemical in the wrong place at the wrong time.

Nothing could be more damaging than what the modern commercial farmer does when he tries to boost his yield by dumping inorganic nutrients (fertilizer) on top of his organic soil. His plants may grow faster for awhile, but eventually his soil dies, because nutrient salts have inhibited the action of the soil's micro-organisms. After a few years his soil is little more than something for his underfed plants to stand around in.

To make matters worse, rain washes a large amount of this fertilizer off the farmer's fields. It enters our creeks and rivers and ends up in our lakes. It does not poison them, but it does overfertilize them. Algae and water plants thrive on it, and they multiply on the surface of the water, blocking light to the lower regions and eventually killing underwater plant and animal life.

Detergents cause the same problem, because they are such terrific fertilizers – the more phosphates the better. Grandma really did know something when she dumped her wash-water on the garden. When you flush your high-phosphate detergent down the drain into the sewage system, you are adding to overfertilization and choking marine life.

In the midst of this we are presented with hydroponics, an environmentally sound growing method where water and nutrients are recycled until they are used up by the plants. Nothing is wasted, and nothing ends up in our rivers and lakes. Your healthy hydroponic plants will tell you that you are doing something right.

Year-Round Gardening

Almost anyone can make things grow outside in summer, but you will find that your hydroponic plants will both outgrow and outproduce their soil-bound cousins. This is partly because they don't have to expend a lot of energy sending out roots to seek nutrients; consequently, they have more energy left for growing.

Hydroponics gives you yet another edge over soil gardeners. They can't go away on vacations when the good weather comes without arranging for the watering and weeding of their gardens. If you have bought or built a hydroponic system that waters automatically, away you go. If it rains or doesn't rain while you're away, so what?

During winter, your hydroponic garden will produce tomatoes, lettuce, cucumbers and whatever other healthful green foods you choose just when their cost is highest and their natural vitamins are most needed. It's a cheery sight to see your vegetables, herbs and flowers sitting fat and happy under a growlight, some ready for harvesting, when the snow is blowing outside. Remember, too, that your planters and plants will act as natural humidifiers for the dry indoor air of winter.

Come spring, you move your portable hydroponic unit outdoors again onto a balcony, porch, patio or into a greenhouse to take full advantage of natural sunlight. Because you have already started your garden indoors under lights, and because it is out of the range of spring ground frost, you can get your first delicious hydroponic tomato two months earlier than your dirt-farming neighbours.

Hydroponic Herbs

Not long ago, herbs grew in every garden and were sold by every greengrocer, but all we seem to use today is parsley as a garnish. Whatever happened to fresh chives, tarragon, basil and sage? We used to know that herbs were natural flavour secrets that would give a lift to the simplest budget dish or the most complex gourmet creation. Perhaps we have forgotten because we have become accustomed to dried herbs whose flavours and fragrances have been destroyed by processing. One of the real joys of hydroponics is the rediscovery of fresh kitchen herbs. Once you have used them, you'll never want to be without them again.

Finally, it is worth remembering that for most people hydroponics is a new and exciting science. There is still much to be learned. Don't be afraid to experiment, particularly if you find that something in this or any other book is unsuitable for you. What works for me may not work for you, and what I believe may not hold true in your particular case. What this book seeks is results for you, and the proof of any system or method is what it produces.

CHAPTER 2

Hydroponic Systems: To Buy or Build?

Many people who enjoy working with their hands, making things, gain tremendous satisfaction from what they create and deplore spending money on a manufactured product. To these people, I say study the diagrams given here and enjoy yourselves. There are at least as many others, however, who would rather concentrate on the actual growing of hydroponic plants and who would prefer to buy a system that they know will work.

One of the wonderful aspects of hydroponics is that there are no limits to the inventiveness of the builder or even the buyer of a system. Try anything that you think will work. If it doesn't, you can always alter your procedure, and you will have gained valuable information in the process. Even the most knowledgeable user is constantly trying new methods, different nutrients, many varieties of plant life and wide ranging applications of all the necessary components of hydroponics. If there is a single word that sums up the best approach to hydroponics, it is *experimentation*.

If you decide to build your own system, remember that hydroponics is more a science than an art. To get satisfactory results from a homemade system, much more is required than a box to hold plant life.

There are four approaches to hydroponic gardening:
1. Growing outdoors as farmers do but using a hydroponic system rather than soil
2. Growing hydroponically indoors
3. A combination of these two, the year-round garden
4. Growing hydroponically in a greenhouse.

The more you substitute for nature, the more complicated these methods become. When plants are removed from their natural environment, as in indoor gardening, then all aspects of that environment have to be duplicated by artificial or technical means. The important thing to recognize in any of these methods is what is taken away and what needs to be replaced. There is no substitute for natural sunlight, for instance, although there are adequate replacements. This is why I recommend that your year-round garden be portable so that it can be moved outside in summer.

Chapter 3 deals extensively with nutrients, because when growing hydroponically this is the most obvious part of the environment we are removing. Should you decide to confine your growing only to the outdoors, then you needn't know a great deal about lighting, temperature and humidity controls, pollination, or any other scientific matters other than nutrients. However, the remaining three approaches do require a working knowledge of all these things. Simply put, pay attention to the environment around your crop, or you won't have a crop. For example, I have received hundreds of letters and phone calls from people saying that they had numerous flowers on their vines indoors, but that the flowers died and fell off before any fruit formed. Their answers to a few questions told me that they knew nothing about pollination or cross-pollination. These are simple tasks that wind and insects usually do, but when the plants are moved indoors, the individual must take over.

There is no reason to be intimidated by *pollination* and other rather scientific terms; the procedures are simple, and they are covered fully in Chapter 10. The point is that you do have to know how. Hydroponics is a science and there is a considerable amount of knowledge that must be acquired. For these reasons, I usually suggest a manufactured system to the novice who chooses to grow a year-round garden or indoors exclusively. The reason is simple: if you start growing hydroponically with a system that is only partially effective, when you start having problems it is more difficult to ascertain whether the trouble is with the system, the quality of nutrient or the environment. You know a manufactured system works, and any problems you encounter will be environmental. You can therefore concentrate your learning in the area of the plants' requirements. Once you have conquered the biological approach to hydroponics, you will have a much better understanding of just what it is you are trying to accomplish and you will have definite ideas about how you wish to go about it.

The person who spends thirty dollars making a simple hydroponic system may discover that seven days a week, three times a day, he or she must be available to pour nutrient over the aggregate. For the busy city-dweller, this could be a hassle. Should our hypothetical person decide to build a more sophisticated system, then what kind? Where should it be put? Which system is best for that individual? The builder may well get bogged down with questions for which suitable answers can't be found, because hydroponic experience is lacking. Other than giving valuable primary experience to the novice, the money may well have been wasted. For a little more money, he or she could have purchased a workable system, experimented a little, gained biological knowledge, got the "feel" of hydroponics and been ready to branch out to build a system suited to the individual's needs.

I don't mean to downgrade the homebuilt system, as the following diagrams and plans show. These remarks are meant as cautions only, because there is nothing more unfortunate than losing an enthusiastic novice due to problems that might have been solved by starting with a manufactured system.

Simple Hydroponic Systems

When building your own system, keep in mind that there are really only two things you are trying to accomplish. The first is a structure that permits support for the root system, and the second is a method of supplying nutrient and aeration to your plants. Every system must begin by satisfying these two requirements. After these requirements are met what we try to achieve is a more sophisticated and automatic method.

For the simplest systems, all you need is a waterproof container filled with some kind of growing medium or aggregate for root support. Into the aggregate you place seeds or young plants whose roots have been washed of soil. Then you pour a nutrient solution over the aggregate to feed the plants. This is hydroponics!

This simple system is not essentially different from the one used in the Hanging Gardens of Babylon, and in its operation we find that several problems arise. It is these problems and the solutions to them that have resulted in the development of more sophisticated, automated systems.

The first problem concerns just how much nutrient to pour over the aggregate. Assuming that the container is waterproof and that the inside bottom of it can't be seen through the walls or down through the aggregate, it is very difficult to gauge the amount or level of nutrient solution. Without this information, it is quite likely that the plants will be killed by either under or overfilling. The only simple solution to this problem is the use of a see-through container, a transparent inspection window or a float system that will allow a visual check of the nutrient level. Otherwise, you must employ a semi or fully automatic system.

The second problem is how often to pour nutrient over the aggregate. Should you decide to "water" your plants hydroponically as you do your house plants, once or twice a week say, you would probably kill everything. Given similar evaporation rates, the nutrient solution will evaporate from the loose aggregate much more quickly than water from soil. Generally speaking, you would have to supply nutrient to your plants about once a day. This would mean you couldn't even go away for a weekend or your hydroponic plants would begin to suffer. The more simple the system, the more frequently someone will have to be available to add nutrient solution. Anywhere from one to four times a day will be necessary depending on light, temperature, humidity, what is being grown, how large your plants are and the size of your container.

A third problem involves proper aeration for the roots. In soil, worms usually perform this function, except, of course, for house plants. One of the major reasons for using hydroponic aggregate is to permit aeration.

AGGREGATES

Aggregates come in many forms: small rounded stones, broken tiles, crushed stone, perlite, slate chips, vermiculite, expanded oil shale and lava stones. Because the growing medium must perform the two functions of support and aeration, the lighter and more porous it is, the better. Actually, almost anything can be used as an aggregate, but the builders and owners of home systems are more limited than commercial growers in the kinds of materials that they can use. Perlite is a bit light, floats somewhat and builds up heat, so it is not as good as some other materials. Vermiculite holds considerable moisture and this can be a real problem for your plants under certain conditions. Broken tiles or pottery can have sharp edges that might damage root systems. Crushed stones or gravel will likely lack porosity and could have lime bases which would be detrimental to your pH level (see Chapter 4).

Of all these materials, haydite seems to me to be preferable. It is an expanded oil shale that has been processed for agricultural purposes. Like lava stones, it has the advantage of being extremely porous for aeration, while at the same time it is capable of holding satisfactory quantities of water. If not processed, both materials must be washed repeatedly in a bucket until the water runs clear to remove accumulated dust and dirt.

Processed haydite is not available in all areas, so you will probably end up using a locally available material or ordering haydite from one of the suppliers listed at the back of this book. In certain locations, haydite may be sold under other names, such as herculite, and it is worth checking with a dealer to find this out. The one drawback of haydite is that it is heavy and consequently expensive to ship.

If you use gravel, broken tiles or haydite, try to keep the pieces no larger than about three-eighths of an inch. Smaller pieces will not give sufficient aeration, larger pieces will hold insufficient moisture.

DRAINAGE

The strength of nutrient solution used and the frequency with which it is applied are both important, as we have seen, but adequate drainage is absolutely essential. Plant roots can only remain submerged in the nutrient solution for a few hours without air before they begin to suffer.

In the simplest systems, drainage may be achieved by simply pouring off the solution or drilling small, strategically placed holes in the container to allow run-off. Such drainage methods, however, require considerable attention and experimentation, and the more we become involved in hydroponics, the more we look for methods of feeding that are less time-consuming.

There are three basic types of automatic, labour-saving feeding and drainage systems:
1. Drip from above (primarily for commercial applications, not too practical for the home)
2. Flood and drain (or sub-irrigation); see figures 2, 4 and 7
3. Constant flow; see figure 8.
I prefer the third method, because the root system is constantly and gently sprayed with nutrient solution and drainage is almost immediate.

The simplest mechanical means of achieving constant flow is by using either an air pump or a small submersible water pump that draws from a reservoir.

The drip from above method does work; however, the growing medium will have a very moist surface, which will result in algae build-up that not only lacks aesthetic appeal, but also can slow down plant growth. The algae will overgrow the aggregate and reduce aeration. It will also probably use up considerable nutrient. The problem of drainage still has to be solved for this method.

Flood and drain works as well, but it, too, can suffer from an algae problem, and I suspect that it may be a bit of a shock for the roots to be suddenly immersed in nutrient two or three times a day. Perhaps more significantly, it is much more difficult to seed directly into this system than into a constant flow arrangement, since the onrush of solution can float seeds or even seedlings to the surface and then wash them too far below the surface as the level recedes.

Whatever system you use in your homemade hydroponic garden, full consideration must be given to drainage before you begin to build. The drainage properties of the growing medium you intend to use must also be kept in mind. As I mentioned earlier, perlite is a bit too light, but drains quickly. On the other hand, vermiculite has a tendency to become impacted after repeated immersions, doesn't flush as well as other materials and should be changed after every crop to ensure proper use. (As well, the vermiculite you use should have as neutral a pH as possible [see Chapter 4] and no toxic amounts of boron or flourine. If your nursery doesn't know the pH and mineral properties of its vermiculite, contact the manufacturer.) Haydite has excellent drainage properties. You must also determine whether you will be using a growing medium over a drainage medium, such as broken tiles over vermiculite, when devising your building plan. In some instances you may feel that your plants do not have sufficient nutrient solution available immediately after draining or between feedings. If this is the case, try putting a one to two inch layer of vermiculite down first with the rock or gravel on top. The vermiculite will hold sufficient moisture for the roots to grow into.

BUILDING YOUR OWN SYSTEM

The following illustrations are of some fairly simple hydroponic systems. Something to keep in mind when building your own system: always obtain all the parts and materials *before* starting. Otherwise you might find that you have drilled the drainage hole a certain diameter and that you can't find the right size plug to fit it. For such things as pumps, timers and tubing, as well as other materials connected with hydroponics, consult the Resource List at the back of this book.

Figure 2 is probably the simplest hydroponic system you can make. Using 3/4 inch plywood, make a box 7 inches deep, 16 inches wide and 24 inches long (all outside dimensions). Fasten the box with wood screws, allowing for the fact that the contents will be heavy. Drill two 1/2 inch holes on one end wall 1/2 inch from the inside bottom.

Line the inside of the box with polyethelene or fibreglass and fit two removable plugs. On the opposite end from the drainage plugs, a 1 inch strip of plywood can be nailed to the bottom. This will sit the tank on an angle and ensure adequate drainage.

This same system can be made using a plastic dishpan or any other waterproof container. It is essential, however, that any material you use for a hydroponic tank is inert, so that no chemical reaction is passed on into your food chain.

For this system, use a 1 inch deep drainage bed of large pieces of broken pottery or rocks that are approximately 3/4 of an inch in size. The size is important to ensure proper drainage and so that the drain holes don't get plugged with the smaller growing medium.

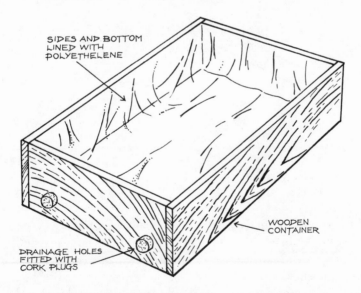

SIDES AND BOTTOM
LINED WITH
POLYETHELENE

WOODEN
CONTAINER

DRAINAGE HOLES
FITTED WITH
CORK PLUGS

Figure 2. A wooden box lined with polyethelene is the simplest hydroponic system to build.

Figure 3 is a manually operated system and is only slightly more automated than that shown in Figure 2.

A pail with a hose attached and sealed at the joints is connected to the growing bed. Raise the pail above the tank to allow a gravity feed of the nutrient solution into the bed. After a half-hour, set the pail on the floor so gravity will drain the solution back into it. The growing bed must be on a table or shelf to allow you to move the pail the proper distance above and below the tank. Be sure that the size of the pail is adequate to flood the system.

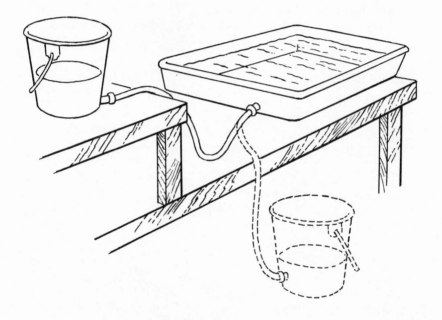

Figure 3. This manually operated system uses a pail and a tank.

The two-tank method in Figure 4 is actually an automated version of Figure 2. Either an additional tank can be built or a large plastic garbage can with a lid can be used. Keep the two tanks close together for maximum efficiency.

Use a small sump pump or a small submersible pump placed in the nutrient solution. Another method for the technically minded would be to seal the nutrient tank and use an aquarium air pump to pressurize the nutrient tank, forcing the solution into the growing bed. This unit should be placed on a timer set at one-half hour durations, three to six times a day.

Only one hole needs to be drilled in the end of the growing bed tank, and this is fitted with a valve and return hose to the nutrient tank.

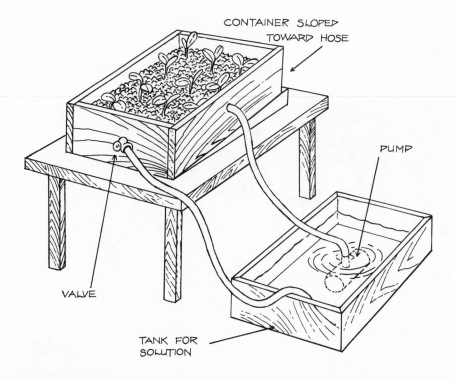

CONTAINER SLOPED
TOWARD HOSE

PUMP

VALVE

TANK FOR
SOLUTION

Figure 4. Two tanks are used in this automated version of the system in Figure 3.

Figure 5 is one answer for the many people who ask what to do with an old aquarium. The two main ingredients to make this kind of system function well are a good strong net and a very light growing medium. Burlap and perlite would be a good combination.

The illustration is self-explanatory, but a few suggestions are in order. When starting seeds or seedlings, the water should barely touch the seed bed. As the roots develop and penetrate the screen into the water, gradually reduce the water level. Roots like air and dislike light, so use your old aquarium pump to aerate the water and cover the outside of the tank with dark material to keep out the light. Make the cover removable, so you can keep a close eye on everything.

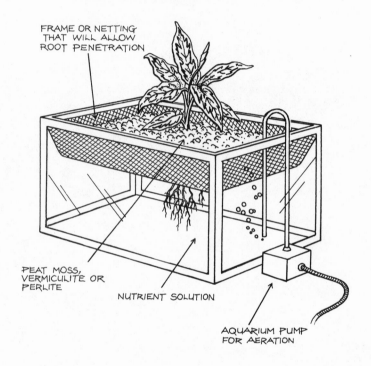

FRAME OR NETTING
THAT WILL ALLOW
ROOT PENETRATION

PEAT MOSS,
VERMICULITE OR
PERLITE

NUTRIENT SOLUTION

AQUARIUM PUMP
FOR AERATION

Figure 5. An unused aquarium can be turned into a hydroponic system.

My suggestion for Figure 6 would be to use a wooden box similar to that shown in Figure 2 for your nutrient reservoir and a large plastic dishpan supported above it on slats of wood.

A very small submersible pump (about 16 to 33 imperial or 20 to 40 U.S. gallons per hour) can be used for this system. Obtain rigid plastic hose, if at all possible, for your distribution line and drill 1/8 inch holes 2 inches apart in it. Drill about twenty 1/8 inch drainage holes in the bottom of the growing tray for final drainage. Insert a 2 inch diameter PVC tube through the growing tray and seal it at the joint. This tube is used for both general and emergency drainage of the nutrient solution.

Your timer could be an industrial unit connected to a wall outlet, which would allow you to regulate several trays at the same time, or you might want to use a portable timer.

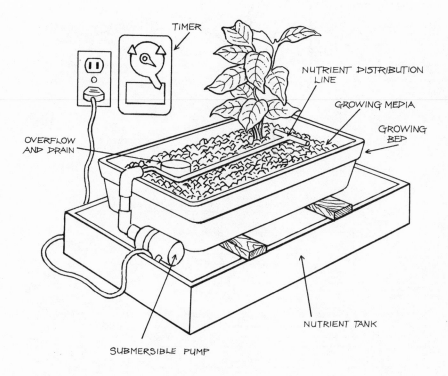

Figure 6. This automated system uses a wooden box for the nutrient tank and a dishpan for the growing bed.

The overflow PVC tube and the timer could be eliminated by using an even smaller submersible pump (about 1-1/2 imperial or two U.S. gallons per hour), which would give you a slow, constant flow method of irrigation. In either case, periodic checks are essential to make sure that the drainage holes in the bottom of the tray are clear.

The complete plans in Figure 7 are meant for the serious enthusiast who wants to build a system from the ground up.

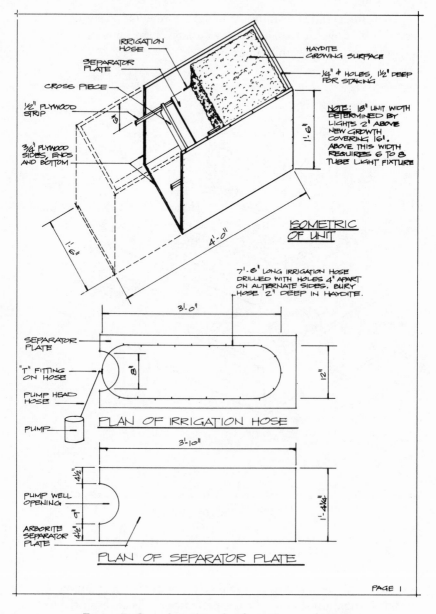

Figure 7. Complete plans for the serious enthusiast.

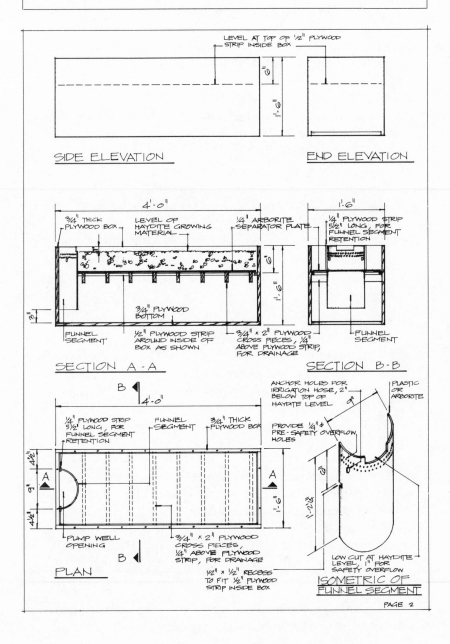

SIDE ELEVATION

END ELEVATION

SECTION A-A

SECTION B-B

PLAN

ISOMETRIC OF FUNNEL SEGMENT

PAGE 2

Materials
1 sheet 3/4 inch plywood
80 oz. fibreglass resin
2-1/2 yards of fibreglass cloth "panelling"
5 yards of fibreglass cloth "joining"
1 NK1 "Little Giant" (No Korode) submersible pump
1 piece of arborite, 16-1/4 by 46 inches
1 piece of arborite, 14-1/4 by 15 inches
10 feet of 1/2 inch plastic tubing (irrigation hose)
6 feet of 1/2 inch plastic tubing (siphon hose for system flushing)
1 box of 2 inch wood screws
1 jar of bonding glue

Substitutions
1. It is easier to use 1 by 3 for the crosspieces than plywood. Simply rip a piece of 1 by 3 for the 1/2 inch strip as well as the retention strips.
2. Look in your Yellow Pages under "Plastics — Vacuum Forming." The chances are that you will be able to buy a piece of plastic .06 thick to use for the separator plate and the funnel segment.

Suggestions
1. Glue all joints before screwing together.
2. Use 5-3/4 inch centres on the crosspieces (i.e., the centre of one hole to the centre of the next is 5-3/4 inches). You will have a much narrower section at the opposite end to the pump well, but there is more growing medium at that end.
3. Apply three coats of fibreglass resin to the interior.
4. After making and fibreglassing the tank, fill it with water to check for leaks.
5. The volume capacity of the growing bed is 2-1/2 cubic feet.
6. Be sure the unit is level.
7. Use a timer that gives you half-hour settings, such as the Intermatic EB41-70.
8. If you see roots in the irrigation tubes or drain holes in the funnel segment, either remove them or cut them out.

Observations
The NK1 pump mentioned in the materials list features a highly corrosion resistant motor housing made of metal and glass-filled

polymer which aids in heat dissipation. The pump is designed to be used in mild acids, alkalies and hard water. The NK1 pumps 171 Imperial or 205 U.S. gallons per hour with a one foot head. These pumps must be submerged to operate.

The fact is that the size of pump you use and where you place your system will have a bearing on irrigation and moisture retention in the growing bed. For these reasons, you will have to keep a close eye on the operation of your system until you can establish precise requirements. If your unit is outdoors in the sun, it will have a much higher evaporation rate on the surface of the growing bed than either indoors or in the shade. In this situation, you may find it necessary to keep your pump on all the time. On the other hand, if you find that the flow of nutrient is too fast (i.e., it floods the unit too often), you can pinch off the header hose a bit with a clamp.

Try using a 2 inch deep bed of at least 1/2 inch diameter vermiculite directly on the separator plate and then top the growing bed with rock or gravel. This will maintain higher water retention nearer the roots and make the total cost of the growing medium less expensive.

IRRIGATION

Because of its efficiency and ease of operation, I prefer a constant flow system, but if the one you build uses the drip from above or flood and drain method, then you must pay careful attention to four requirements:

1. Suitable daily pumping periods
2. Pumping intervals
3. Duration of irrigation
4. Nutrient solution depth.

If you are pumping once a day, you should do it during the warmest part of the day, usually afternoon, the period of greatest plant transpiration. This will help overcome the problem of wilting. If you are pumping twice a day, then maintain this first period and add an early morning feeding. For three times a day, add an early evening period. With an automatic system, it is simple to use a grounded timer (safer than an ungrounded one) to regulate these feedings. If your system is manual, and no one is available after mid-day, then it is better to feed in the morning than at night.

Required pumping intervals depend on a number of factors, such as what you are growing; plant size; water retention, or lack of it, in the growing or drainage medium; and the climate, including temperature and humidity. Tomatoes will require a far greater amount of water than lettuce, for example, and porous stones, more water than vermiculite or perlite. Hot, dry conditions cause more rapid evaporation than a cool and humid atmosphere. Your plants will use greater amounts of water than nutrient, assuming you are using a correct solution, because the nutrient does not evaporate with the water. Therefore, the water requirements of your plants and your aggregate are the prime considerations in calculating pumping intervals. One to six times per day would not be unreasonable.

The most common approach to the duration of irrigation is one half-hour. You should try to drain the system as quickly as possible after this time to prevent possible shock to the roots. If the rate is too slow, the roots will be immersed for too long and there will be a corresponding lack of aeration.

The depth of the nutrient solution depends to a certain extent on the kinds of plants you are growing and their sizes. Both the drip from above and the flood and drain methods give rise to algae growth if the surface is constantly moistened, but bringing the solution level almost to the top is unavoidable when seeds and seedlings are present. In fact, you must be careful to raise the level high enough to moisten the seeds, but not so high that they are covered completely, only to be washed deeply into the aggregate during drainage. If algae starts to grow on the surface of your growing bed, you can eliminate it by providing more aeration to the top one inch of the bed, by making the surface less moist, or by removing the light source (if possible) for a few days. I do not recommend the use of algaecides such as the ones used in fish aquariums and ponds. Permanganese and other similar substances are poisonous and can be transferred into your food chain.

Manufactured Systems

To give some idea of the differences between homemade and commercially available systems, the following drawings show constant flow, manufactured hydroponic units. The use of such systems, particularly as a novice, will assist you in finding out about hydroponics and in getting early results.

Figure 8 is a semi-commercial type of system, manufactured by Canadian Hydrogardens, Ancaster, Ontario. The unit is designed to fit into an eight by ten or ten by twelve foot greenhouse, or in a backyard in southern climates. Each bed is thirty-two by one hundred and eight inches and is fed by a nutrient reservoir connected to a timer and pump. The beds themselves are made of rigid plastic and set into wooden frames.

When growing a wide variety of vegetables in a single bed of a system like this, it is more difficult to control nutrient quality and pH level. For this reason, it would be better to try and divide your vegetables into at least two groups with similar nutrient and pH requirements before planting.

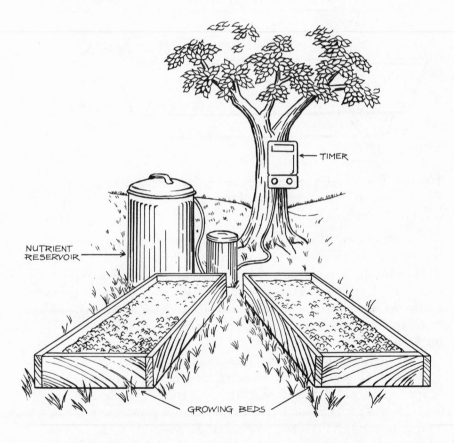

Figure 8. The "Hydrogarden" manufactured system is designed to fit into a greenhouse or in a backyard in southern climates.

Figures 9 and 10 show the commercially made "City Green" home system. The tank is one solid piece of light and durable injected foam urethane with two partitions for added strength. The separator plate sits on a one-half inch ledge surrounding the perimeter and the partitions.

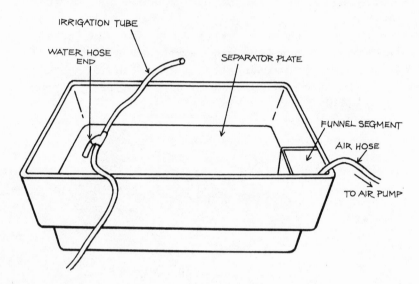

Figure 9. The "City Green" home system before the drainage and growing media have been added.

A one inch thick layer of vermiculite is set into the tank on top of the separator plate. This acts as a drainage medium. On top of this is added three-quarters of an inch of growing medium (expanded oil shale) and the perforated plastic tubes are set in place. Another three-quarters of an inch of growing medium is placed on top of the irrigation hoses, partly to anchor them, and partly to prevent an algae build-up on the surface.

An air hose is attached to an aquarium pump that is set on the floor, and it is inserted into the funnel segment down into the tank. The hose is then threaded through the partitions (a one inch hole drilled in the bottom of each one) and inserted into a larger plastic (water) hose running up through the separator plate where the perforated irrigation tubes are attached. The air travelling through the air hose and entering the water hose acts with a venturi effect to lift the nutrient solution from the bottom of the tank up into the growing bed.

The separator plate has a few one-eighth inch holes drilled in it to allow drainage. Drainage is assisted by the fact that there are raised dimples along the ledge that surrounds the inside of the tank and supports the plate. Together these features permit proper drainage and recirculation of the nutrient solution.

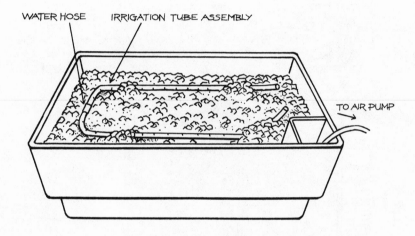

Figure 10. The "City Green" home system before the final layer of growing medium has been placed over the irrigation hoses.

CHAPTER 3

Nutrients

While you are deciding whether to build or buy a home hydroponic unit, it would be a good idea to do a little studying about nutrients. No matter what kind of system you choose, nutrients will be an integral part of your success, because your plants must be constantly supplied with food.

Using the formulae given in this chapter, you will be able to mix your own nutrients in either large or small amounts. As in Chapter 2, however, I recommend that the novice begin with a commercially available, pre-mixed nutrient at least until a feel for hydroponics has been developed.

Nature does a lot of the work in soil gardening, although often not perfectly, or farmers would not have to use fertilizers. Almost all soil has some nutrients in it, but when you are growing hydroponically, you are taking over from nature, and in many instances it is possible for you to improve the quality of nutrients supplied.

Homemade Nutrients

The most common type of homemade nutrient is one made from fertilizer salts. These salts are available in bulk from agricultural agencies, plant food suppliers, some nurseries and gardening stores, and chemical suppliers. The only problem with this approach is that you usually have to buy some of these salts in twenty-five to fifty pound bags, and unless you are growing in extensive hydroponic gardens, such quantities make the whole thing rather cumbersome and expensive. Even so, for the adventurous, or for the person who simply wants to know, the following information should give a good general knowledge of these materials.

Fertilizer Salts	Elements Supplied
Ammonium phosphate	Nitrogen and Phosphorus
Ammonium sulphate	Nitrogen and Sulphur
Calcium nitrate	Nitrogen and Calcium
Potassium nitrate*	Nitrogen and Potassium
Sodium nitrate	Nitrogen
Potassium sulphate*	Potassium and Sulphur
Superphosphate*	Phosphorus and Calcium
Calcium sulphate*	Calcium and Sulphur
Magnesium sulphate* (Epsom salts)	Magnesium and Sulphur
Ferrous sulphate*	Iron
Manganese chloride	Manganese
Zinc sulphate	Zinc
Copper sulphate	Copper
Boric acid powder*	Boron

The salts marked with an asterisk are the best to work with where there are other, similar salts available, because they have superior properties, such as better solubility, cost, storage life, and stability. Potassium chloride, for example, could be used rather than potassium sulphate, but if applied for more than a few days, the chlorine in the mix could prove harmful to your plants. This is especially true since there is likely to be chlorine in your water in the first place. Magnesium nitrate could be substituted for magnesium sulphate, but it hardly seems worthwhile to use a more expensive material for the cheap and readily available epsom salts. Ferric citrate has to be dissolved in hot water, as opposed to cold for ferrous sulphate.

In addition to the three key elements of nitrogen (N), phosphorus (P) and potassium (K) that are essential to all plant growth, there should be at least ten trace elements present in your nutrient. These are: sulphur, iron, manganese, zinc, copper, boron, magnesium, calcium, chlorine and molybdenum. The following list gives the specific function of each one in plant growth.

Element	Function
Nitrogen	Necessary for the production of leaves and in stem growth. An essential ingredient in building plant cells.
Phosphorus	Required in the development of flowers and fruits and aids in the growth of healthy roots.
Potassium	Used by plant cells during the assimilation of the energy produced by photosynthesis.
Sulphur	Assists in the production of plant energy and heightens the effectiveness of phosphorus.
Iron	Vital in the production of chlorophyll.
Manganese	Aids in the absorption of nitrogen. An essential component in the energy transference process.
Zinc	An essential component in the energy transference process.
Copper	Needed in the production of chlorophyll.
Boron	Required in minute amounts, but it is not yet known how the plant uses it.
Magnesium	One of the components of chlorophyll, magnesium also is involved in the process of distributing phosphorus throughout the plant.
Calcium	Encourages root growth and helps the plant absorb potassium.
Chlorine	Required for photosynthesis.
Molybdenum	Assists in some chemical reactions.

There are hundreds of different nutrient formulae, but as long as the elements are present in balanced amounts, you have little to worry about. Trying to choose the best formula is a meaningless task, since many of the experts disagree. In the final analysis, your decision will probably be based on cost, availability and your own preferences. However, plants do require different nutrients on different days, at different times of the day and under different conditions. Unless you did an exhaustive test every day, it would be impossible to determine just what the plant requires at any one time. This is why it is essential to provide the plant with a balanced nutrient solution all the time and leave it up to the plant to use what it requires.

As it is used here, the term "balanced" simply means that the nutrient contains the proper ratio of elements to satisfy the maximum requirements of the plant. This is done by calculating the molecular weights of the elements and compounds used in a particular formula. The ratio is arrived at by calculating the parts per million concentration of each element. Scientifically, this description may be somewhat inaccurate because of its simplicity. In fact, this may occur a few times in my discussions of the more scientific aspects of hydroponics, but I believe it is better to simplify for the novice and let the reader turn to more scientific books when he wants to experiment.

The plant will absorb what it needs through the small hairs on the ends of its roots. This selectivity makes it impossible to overfeed your plants in hydroponics. Don't forget, though, that if you mix too high a concentration of nutrient in the water you are using, the plant will be unable to absorb sufficient water. Salts need to dilute themselves, and if the concentration is too high, the plant will start giving off water instead of ingesting it, and the result will be a plant that dehydrates itself.

The following are six workable nutrient formulae. They are based on a 100 Imperial (120 American) gallon quantity. If you plan to use less than a 100 gallon solution, use 2 tablespoons of the powder mix to one gallon of water. Each formula is translated into ounces rather than setting out complicated chemical equations based on atomic weights and parts per million.

Formula 1

Sodium nitrate	12-1/2 ounces
Potassium sulphate	4 ounces
Superphosphate	5 ounces
Magnesium sulphate	3-1/2 ounces

Combine with trace elements and 100 gallons (120 American gallons) of water.

Formula 2

Sodium nitrate	10 ounces
Calcium nitrate	10 ounces
Potassium sulphate	10 ounces
Superphosphate	15 ounces
Magnesium sulphate	5 ounces

Combine with trace elements and 100 gallons (120 American gallons) of water.

Formula 3

Potassium nitrate	16 ounces
Ammonium sulphate	6 ounces
Superphosphate	6-1/2 ounces
Magnesium sulphate	5 ounces

Combine with trace elements and 100 gallons (120 American gallons) of water.

Formula 4

Sodium nitrate	8 ounces
Ammonium phosphate	1-3/4 ounces
Potassium sulphate	4 ounces
Calcium nitrate	1 ounce
Magnesium sulphate	3-1/2 ounces

Combine with trace elements and 100 gallons (120 American gallons) of water.

Formula 5

Ammonium sulphate	16 ounces
Potassium sulphate	6 ounces
Superphosphate	6-1/2 ounces
Magnesium sulphate	5 ounces

Combine with trace elements and 100 gallons (120 American gallons) of water.

Formula 6

Ammonium sulphate	1-1/2 ounces
Potassium nitrate	9 ounces
Monocalcium phosphate	4 ounces
Magnesium sulphate	6 ounces
Calcium sulphate	7 ounces

Combine with trace elements and 100 gallons (120 American gallons) of water.

The trace elements that are added to these formulae must be mixed separately. Two recipes are given below. Use a mortar and pestle to grind to a very fine powder.

Trace Elements No. 1

Iron sulphate	1 ounce
Manganese sulphate	1 teaspoon
Boric acid powder	1 teaspoon
Zinc sulphate	1/2 teaspoon
Copper sulphate	1/2 teaspoon

These ingredients should be mixed well and stored dry. Use 1/2 teaspoon per 100 gallons (120 American gallons) of water, or dissolve 1/2 teaspoon in one quart (1.2 American quarts) of water and use one liquid ounce to 3 gallons (3.6 American gallons) of nutrient solution. Throw the rest of the quart away; be sure not to use any portion of the remainder of this quart of trace element solution. Any trace element mix cannot be kept in a liquid state and retain its quality, so don't keep this solution beyond one day.

Trace Elements No. 2

This formula has two separate components. They should be mixed dry and stored separately until ready for use.

A

Fe 330, iron chelate	2 teaspoons
Manganese chloride	1/2 teaspoon
Boric acid powder	1-1/4 teaspoon

These three ingredients should be dissolved in one gallon (1.2 American gallons) of water. Add 5 liquid ounces to 10 gallons (12 American gallons) of nutrient solution.

B

Copper sulphate	1/4 teaspoon
Zinc sulphate	1/2 teaspoon

Dissolve these two elements in one gallon (1.2 American gallons) of water and add 10 drops to the same 10 gallons of nutrient solution.

Many hydroponic gardeners will not need a hundred gallons of nutrient solution, but it is an easy matter to calculate the weight to the quantity you require based on the hundred gallon solution figures. In Formula 1, for instance, the total weight of fertilizer salts is thirty-two ounces to one hundred gallons of water. If you need twenty-five gallons of nutrient solution, you would apply eight ounces of salts plus the required amount of trace elements.

It is essential that all calculations by weight be accurate. Care must also be taken that the proper compatible "chemicals" are used and that they are properly mixed. The substances listed for each formula differ greatly, because, although the elements themselves are the same, the salts from which they are released vary in each composition. Occasionally, all the trace elements are not necessary in a separate application, for many of the salts being used contain some of the trace elements as impurities.

The two trace elements (micronutrients) chlorine and molybdenum require a brief discussion. Frequently, chlorine is not added to a trace element formula, because there is usually enough found in public works water systems. Some books mention molybdenum as a micronutrient, others ignore it completely. The reason it is often skipped is that only .02 parts per million are required, an amount so minute that if enough is not present as a salt impurity, then the danger of adding too much to your nutrient is not worth the risk. Besides, plants have the ability to compensate for a molybdenum deficiency, should one exist.

Ready-Made Nutrients

If you have a very small hydroponic unit, whether homemade or bought, you may not feel that you wish to go to all the bother of making your own nutrients. If this is so, it is quite easy to obtain commercial nutrients in from one to twenty-five pound containers.

Ordinarily, the novice hydroponic gardener knows relatively little of chemistry. Using a pre-mixed nutrient is the most straightforward way of assuring that your plants get a balanced diet. There are good hydroponic nutrients on the market that have all the necessary trace elements. They can be bought at many large nurseries and plant stores or from some of the suppliers listed at the back of this book. If it becomes necessary to adjust your nutrient at some point, it is certainly easier for the grower who lacks chemical knowledge to be using an identifiable ready-made nutrient.

When purchasing commercial hydroponic nutrient, its quality is identified with three digits separated by hyphens, such as 20-20-20. These numbers represent the percentage by weight of the three main elements present: nitrogen, phosphorus and potassium. There are various nutrients on the market that have different ratios, but, generally speaking, they are all well balanced. Commercial nutrients have their drawbacks, however, because most users of soilless gardens are growing a wide variety of vegetables at the same time, and it is impossible to provide a specific plant food for each different vegetable at each stage of its growth. The only answer would be to have a different type of plant in each container, a solution to the problem that would often prove too expensive and space-consuming. When using a commercial nutrient, I have found it a good idea to add a little 10-52-10 plant food, or another plant food with a high middle number, to the existing nutrient at the stage of bud development in vegetables such as cucumbers or tomatoes. Any nutrient with a very high middle number will do. The nitrogen and potassium (soluble potash) represented by the first and third numbers will simply provide the plant with more of these elements if it needs them, but the increased amount of phosphorus will aid in the development of buds and flowers. To your existing nutrient solution add one-half teaspoon per gallon (1.2 American gallons). You should begin this treatment when buds first start to develop and for as long as this development continues.

Formula Adjustments

Whether yours is a homemade or a commercial nutrient, there will be times when adjustments are necessary. Formula adjustments are probably the trickiest part of hydroponics, and caution should be used at all times or you could destroy your entire crop in a matter of days.

If you are using a well-balanced, commercial nutrient and a correction is necessary due to a deficiency that you can't identify, a foliar spray may be the answer. You can make the spray from a *very* diluted mix of nutrient and water. The easiest method would be to make up one quart of nutrient solution at regular strength and then dilute it with water to a one-to-seven or even a one-to-ten ratio. Use a mister and spray the diluted solution on the leaves of the affected plants once a day for several days. The leaves will absorb it quickly and spreading of the symptoms should be reduced greatly in a short period of time. A foliar spray can probably solve many of your trace element deficiency problems.

A large-scale commercial grower will analyze the leaf tissue of his plants every few days and make adjustments as necessary. Because this requires a great deal of knowledge, time and money for equipment, it is impractical for the modest home grower. In fact, it needn't be all that important in a home system where you are experimenting with hydroponics, raising relatively small crops and changing your nutrient solution every three to four weeks. If you spend ten to fifteen minutes a day with your system, you will find that in a few months you will be able to read the signals given by your plants and be ready to make necessary changes to the nutrient. Like anything else that's worthwhile, tuning in to your plants takes time, but the rewards are great.

Figure 11. A foliar spray applied with a mister can usually solve many trace element deficiency problems.

Water Supply

Ordinarily, your home water supply will be quite satisfactory for hydroponics, but a few cautions should be given. Water from a water softener should not be used, as it will be far too alkaline. On the other hand, rain or distilled water would be fine, providing a reliable and inexpensive supply could be maintained. Tapwater is average and it will generally contain small amounts of trace elements that the plant can use if it requires them. Water that is too pure may have to be supplemented with slight increases of some trace elements, especially calcium and magnesium. If the water is very hard, you will need less calcium and magnesium but probably more iron, because iron becomes less available to the plant as the hardness of the water increases. For these reasons, it is a good idea to have an analysis done on your water supply at your local utility. If you obtain your water from a well or source other than a Public Works Department, you can contact your nearest Agricultural Department for an address to send in a water sample. Any analysis should include the content of calcium, magnesium, iron sulphate, chloride and carbonate. In any case, it's probably worthwhile to know what you are drinking and using in your home.

Many apartments and modern homes are hot and dry, and you should bear in mind that these conditions can cause as much as a fifty per cent decrease in the need for potassium. Under very humid conditions, where the light level is lower, your plants will require more potassium — as much as twice the normal amount. This is because photosynthesis is more difficult with a lower light level and potassium is necessary for photosynthesis.

Common Nutrient Deficiency Symptoms

One of the main problems in attempting to determine the cause of a specific nutrient deficiency symptom is that almost everything sounds the same. In fact, this is not so; there are small differences in each problem. Like a doctor, you must attempt to isolate the symptoms and study the case history. Even if you are only able to reduce the possible causes to two or three at first, you can then isolate the symptoms, weigh the factors leading up to the problem, further reduce the possibilities to one or two at most, and take remedial action. The following chart will help you do this.

Element	Symptom
Nitrogen	Small, stunted plants with very large root systems; leaves smaller and lighter in colour than normal; slow growth. Paleness will start at the tips of the lower leaves. If this deficiency continues, the foliage will continue to develop, but stems will be spindly, sappy and soft, flowering will be delayed, small fruit will grow and the plant will be more susceptible to disease.
Phosphorus	Stunted plants with dark, dull and sometimes discoloured leaves, unusually hard stems, poor root system, and very little branching. Attacks lower, more mature leaves first. Occurs especially when nitrogen level is low.
Potassium	In early stages, yellowing and curling of older leaves. Newer leaves will begin to droop. Older leaves then become blotchy and scorched. Flowers are lackluster, and stems are soft. The plant will be more susceptible to diseases such as mildew and rust.
Calcium	Underdeveloped roots are the first to be effected. Younger leaves will be immobile and their edges will curl. Plants will be stunted and have dark, crinkly leaves. (See blossom end rot, Chapter 13.)
Magnesium	Symptoms do not appear until the deficiency is well established. The plant will be stunted. Leaf veins will stay green while the remainder of the leaf turns yellow. Brown spots will appear and then the plant will dry out. Flowers will be slow to develop, if at all. Flowers that do grow will be lackluster.
Iron	Tips of new leaves will become either pale or yellow, and this will spread inward. The leaf will likely turn blotchy from a lack of green pigment, eventually turning brown and drying out.
Manganese	Poor blooming, weak growth. Leaves may turn yellow or blotchy.
Boron	Brittle stems, and immobile new leaves with brown tips.
Zinc	Growth will be stunted.

It is not necessarily true that you will encounter any or all of these imbalance problems. Because of your particular situation or environment, however, you may find that from time to time specific problems will arise. It is worth repeating that the watchword of hydroponics is experimentation, as much in problem solving as in developing a system that suits your needs.

Toxicity

The symptoms listed in this chapter are symptoms of element deficiencies. On the other hand, a toxic (poisonous) situation can be created when one or more elements are being supplied in excessive amounts. It is very unlikely that such a situation will occur if the reader follows with reasonable accuracy any of the hundreds of formulae available in books. It seems unnecessary to load the novice with information on toxicity that will likely never be needed. However, the real seeker of knowledge should consult *Hydroponic Food Production,* by Howard M. Resh.

Hints for Storing and Making Nutrients

1. Store all fertilizer salts, trace elements and nutrients in airtight containers, away from air and moisture.
2. When making your own nutrient, use a large, clean bowl for mixing. The best instruments for crushing any crystals into a fine powder are a mortar and pestle; the chemist's type is the finest, but kitchen supply stores also carry adequate ones.
3. Grind trace elements separately and add these last, stirring everything together very carefully.
4. Try to make sure all powders are completely dissolved in water before application to your hydroponic system.

CHAPTER 4

Hydroponics and pH Level

Most people are familiar with the term pH, even if it is only a dim memory from high school biology. Few bother to investigate what it means, beause it is unimportant to them in their daily lives. Becoming involved in hydroponics, however, demands that you acquire a working knowledge of pH. The term sounds scientific and difficult but, in fact, pH simply means the relative acidity or alkalinity of a solution. In hydroponics, we are interested in determining the pH level of water before nutrient is added to it, making adjustments if necessary, and then checking the level of the nutrient periodically.

Determining pH

If we take a scale of 1 to 14, the centre point, or neutral position, is 7. Everything above neutral is alkaline and everything below is acidic. To determine accurate pH levels, each whole number is divided into ten parts. Thus we have 6.8, 6.9, 7.0, 7.1, 7.2 and so on. When growing several kinds of vegetables or herbs in one container, you will probably do best in the slightly acidic range of 5.6 to 6.5, because it is within this range that the nutrients are most available to the plants. For instance, at 7.0, which is outside the most suitable range for vegetables, plants are still capable of taking up such elements as nitrogen, phosphorus and potassium. At this level, though, the trace elements are becoming lost to the plants; the amounts of iron, manganese, boron, copper, zinc and molybdenum are generally cut in half. So when the pH is above 7, be on the lookout for trace element problems, rather than those caused by the macronutrients nitrogen, phosphorus and potassium.

The two most common methods of determining pH level are by indicator (litmus) paper and by indicator solution. Each method is simple to use, readily available and sufficiently accurate for the home grower. It is rather unlikely that your water supply will fluctuate in pH, but if it does, a level check every two or three days may be necessary; otherwise once a week will suffice.

Many areas have a water pH of 7.0 to 8.2. A good commercial nutrient will likely have a small effect on this figure, pulling it down closer to the desirable 5.6 to 6.5 range. With frequent changes of nutrient solution, pH should not become a major problem.

In addition to the water pH and the effect of nutrient upon it, there are two other important factors to consider. One is the hardness of the water, and the second is the pH of the growing medium in combination with water. If you failed to get a water analysis when working with nutrients (see Chapter 3), you should certainly get one when determining pH. The analysis will tell you how hard your water is.

Other variables affecting pH are climate, what plants you are growing and how much nutrient each plant uses. There are many combinations of these variables, which you will learn through experience. The hobbyist who does not wish to become too involved in the complications of pH will still get decent crops. Needless to say, the experience of continuous growing will gradually teach you a great deal about this subject.

Figure 12. A litmus paper test is an easy way to determine pH.

Adjusting the pH Level

If your nutrient solution falls outside the 5.6 to 6.5 range, try the following remedies:

1. To a solution that is too alkaline add one tablespoon of white vinegar per three gallons (3.6 American gallons) of water and check the pH level every eight hours. The waiting period has to do with the fact that it sometimes takes a few hours for the vinegar to work through the solution. Using vinegar is only a temporary measure. On the whole it is too unstable to be satisfactory for more than a few days.

2. To a solution that is too acidic simply add baking soda. It is difficult to specify the quantity here due to wide variations in water quality and nutrient balance. You might try one table-spoon to three gallons of water. Experience will be the best guide.

3. If you want to be more accurate, try adding phosphoric acid to a solution that is too alkaline. It is considerably less dangerous than the acids commonly used by commercial growers. Don't let the word "acid" frighten you; phosphoric acid used carefully is almost harmless. Just be sure to wash it off right away with baking soda and water if you spill any on yourself.

   During recent tests on water with a pH of 8.0 and a hardness factor of 136 parts per million, 0.1 millilitres of phosphoric acid were used to one gallon of water. The pH was reduced to 6.8. For example, if the hardness was 172 parts per million, one would add about 0.15 millilitres of the acid. There are 5.0 millilitres to 1 teaspoon and 15 drops to 1.0 millilitre. Therefore, in adding 0.1 millilitres you are using one and a half drops. Again, let your solution mix with the acid and check the pH about eight hours later and again twenty-four hours later.

Yet another way of adjusting the pH level is through the use of dolmitic lime. It will not only raise the level of your nutrient from acidic to more alkaline, but it also makes potassium more available to your plants. In addition, lime provides the calcium and magnesium which may be lacking in your water supply.

The best way to apply dolmitic lime is to sprinkle it evenly throughout your drainage or growing medium. If you are using a layer of vermiculite for drainage under the growing medium, this is the place to apply it. On the other hand, when using a single growing medium of rock or other substance, you should sprinkle the lime in a thin layer at about half the depth of the aggregate. One tablespoon per two square feet should be enough, but as in many other hydroponic "rules," you will have to gain experience to determine the exact amount that is required in your system. Lime should not be added continuously; it should be applied only when you are certain your plants need it, or after dismantling and cleaning the system thoroughly.

Run pH tests using the lime with combinations of water, nutrient and growing media and record the information in a log. You may find that your growing medium is very alkaline, if you are using some form of lava stones or expanded oil shale. In such a situation, be careful of the amount of lime you use.

Plant Preferences

There are vegetables that are classified as acidic lovers and those that do well under more alkaline conditions. Should you develop your hydroponic system to the point where you have several tanks in a greenhouse, for instance, and you have a different herb or vegetable in each tank, then it may be advisable to investigate and follow up on the individual requirements of each plant. The following list gives the pH preferences of common vegetables, herbs and fruits.

Bean, lima	6.0-7.0	Kohlrabi	6.0-7.5
Bean, pole	6.0-7.5	Leek	6.0-8.0
Beet	6.0-7.5	Lettuce	6.0-7.0
Broccoli	6.0-7.0	Mustard	6.0-7.5
Brussels sprouts	6.0-7.5	Okra	6.0-7.5
Cabbage	6.0-7.5	Onion	6.0-7.0
Cantaloupe	6.0-7.5	Parsley	5.0-7.0
Carrot	5.5-7.0	Parsnip	5.5-7.0
Cauliflower	5.5-7.5	Pea	6.0-7.5
Celery	5.8-7.0	Pepper	5.5-7.0
Chicory	5.0-6.5	Radish	6.0-7.0
Chive	6.0-7.0	Sage	5.5-6.5
Cucumber	5.5-7.0	Soybean	6.0-7.0
Eggplant	5.5-6.5	Spinach	6.0-7.5
Endive	5.8-7.0	Squash, crookneck	6.0-7.5
Garlic	5.5-8.0	Squash, hubbard	5.5-7.0
Kale	6.0-7.5	Strawberry	5.0-6.5

Swiss chard	6.0-7.5	Turnip	5.5-6.8
Thyme	5.5-7.0	Watercress	6.0-8.0
Tomato	5.5-7.5	Watermelon	5.5-6.5

When growing combinations of vegetables, a good pH range is 5.6 to 6.5. A good range for growing herbs only is 5.6 to 7.0. If you are growing combinations of vegetables and herbs try to maintain a 6.0 to 6.5 range.

Water Supply

As mentioned earlier, most communities have an alkaline water supply. Be sure and safe; have your water checked. Try collecting rain water, if your supply is of poor quality. Some adjustments will be necessary in areas where the water is not relatively neutral. Pure water with no mineral content may require additions of calcium and magnesium. Using the table in Chapter 3, keep a close eye on your plants for mineral problems, particularly iron deficiencies.

Adjustments in pH level are more difficult when using a commercial nutrient, because you can more easily upset the nutrient balance. Consult a local agricultural expert if you feel the need. Perhaps for those growers with water problems, the only solution is homemade nutrients, but I would try other ways first.

Some Simple pH Tests

Here are a few tests you can run that will help you understand some of the prime pH variables, as well as gain some experience:

1. Do a pH test on your water
2. Do a pH test on your water adding nutrient
3. Do a pH test on your growing medium after adding water
4. Do a pH test on your water, nutrient and growing medium combined
5. Try to obtain phosphoric acid (see the Resource List at the back of this book) and do tests 1 to 4 again, but in each case add the required amount of acid to obtain the range you desire.

Remember that you should always adjust the pH of your water before adding nutrient. If necessary, adjust again after adding the nutrient. In all cases of pH adjustment, record your test results and reading in a log (see page 131). This information should give you most of the basics you will require to maintain a satisfactory pH level.

CHAPTER 5

Climate

Climate plays a vital role in the growing of plant life indoors. But for a home hydroponic hobbyist, it would be both impractical and very expensive to try to control climatic conditions totally. This would necessitate keeping a tight climatic rein on the entire house, or at least a sealed-off room.

The three main factors to consider are light, temperature and humidity, factors that you can control to an adequate degree for indoor growing. Given proper attention, the control of these three aspects will definitely increase your crop yield.

Light

Photosynthesis is the process whereby a plant utilizes certain colour wavelengths of light to manufacture energy. This energy is then used by the plant as fuel for growth. It is obvious to all of us that plants need some light each day in order to survive, and science has shown us that major photosynthesis activity takes place when the red and blue wavelengths are present. All plants have different light intensity requirements, ranging from a far corner of a room to brilliant sunshine.

If you decide to grow hydroponic vegetables indoors, you must use artificial lights, because, in order to fruit, vegetables require high light levels to develop vast amounts of energy. Alternately, a good-sized window with a south or west exposure will probably allow you to grow herbs, leaf lettuce and possibly Tiny Tim tomatoes without lights. Remember, though, that too much direct sunlight through a glass

49

window magnifies into an inordinate amount of heat that could ruin your crop. A shade of some sort should be used during the period of most intense sun. Beyond these three crops, lights are certainly better and in most cases necessary; but even when using them, it is a good idea to place your hydroponic unit near a window.

When arranging where to put your hydroponic tanks, or when purchasing a lighting fixture, try to use a light meter. In my experience, the minimum requirement is one thousand foot-candle power.* (One foot-candle power is the amount of light falling on one square foot of space located one foot away from a high quality candle.) It is true that you can grow indoors with less than this amount, but this depends on what you are growing, and certainly most vegetables should have the thousand or more.

For artificial lighting, you may use mercury vapour, sodium vapour, metal halide lamps, tungsten filament or fluorescent. Fluorescent lights are the most popular, and they can be broken down into several groups: Regular High Power Factor (Bi-Pin), High Output and Very High Output. Each is a different type of tube, and they are in ascending order of light output as well as price. Within each type, there is a selection of tubes of differing colour outputs; those that are useful to the indoor gardener are listed below.

Tube	Comments
Cool White	The industry standard, and the least expensive – strong blue, medium red.
Warm White	Medium blue, medium red. Strong yellow and orange give it the appearance of red.
Plant Tubes	Strong blue, strong red. Sold under various brand names, such as *Gro-Lux* and *Agro-Lite*.
Full Spectrum	A new variety, resulting from research in photobiology. Its spectrum is very close to sunlight, with low-level ultraviolet included. This concept looks promising for the future. *Vita-Lite* is the most readily available at present.

* There are two other terms used to measure light intensity that should not confuse you if you run into them in other books. They are "Equivalent Sphere Illumination" and "Lumens." The first term is for a type of light intensity measurement that also takes into account such things as glare, as from a white wall in brilliant sunlight. Lumens refers to the intensity of light at the source. With a few calculations (1 foot candle = 10.8 lx.) this measurement can be converted into foot-candle power, which, as you know, is the intensity of light striking a given position.

The type or combination of types is important, but really depends on what you are growing. A flowering plant requires stronger red than green leaf plants such as lettuce or house plants. Choose your lighting accordingly. One interesting way that this difference turns up is when herbs are grown under a Plant Tube, where they flower much sooner than under a plain Cool White tube. With some herbs, for example those you want to go to seed for later crops, this is an asset, but for others it is not.

The tungsten filament (light bulb) produces a spectrum that starts in yellow and goes through orange to red. It provides none of the blue that is needed for compact leaf growth. It is an efficient space heater, however, it that's what you want. Remember the above points and use the light bulb accordingly.

In their book, *Gardening Indoors Under Lights,* Fred and Jacqueline Kranz suggest that far red in the spectrum is very important and found that it is provided by the incandescent bulb. They also mention that it is essential to maintain a proper ratio of far red to red rays. This was first suggested by Dr. R. J. Downs, a member of the team that made impor-

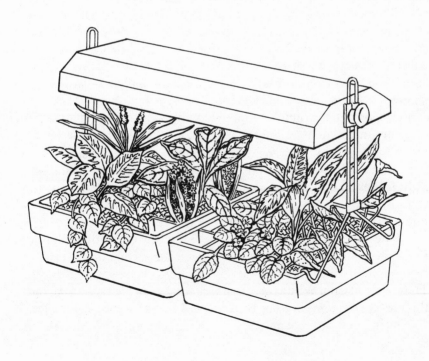

tant discoveries in light spectrum analysis. The ratio of three watts fluorescent to one watt incandescent is the best according to these authors. Minor disparities, if not too marked, are acceptable. Therefore, when using four 40 watt Cool White tubes, you should combine them with two 15 watt incandescent bulbs.

Mercury and sodium vapour lamps are high pressure, high intensity and high priced. They are suitable for large areas of high intensity production. Their spectra are good for certain crops in conjunction with sunlight, as in a commercial greenhouse, but they are somewhat impractical at present for the family-sized, indoor hydroponic garden for two reasons. The first is cost. Many people do not want to spend three hundred dollars at an early stage of their new hobby. The second is the high heat output of these lamps, which in turn causes high temperatures. However, there is no doubt that this type of lighting will be important in the future. Michigan State University, the University of Guelph, the General Electric Company, Agriculture Canada and Washington State University have all been conducting experiments with mercury and sodium vapour lamps. These lights, whose foot-candle power at source almost matches the sun's, could solve the problems of indoor and winter growing of vegetables.

Whatever kind of light you finally select, make sure it does not give off too much heat. Should you, for example, decide to use a flood light, it is important to remember that it produces a high degree of heat. The only effective way to overcome this problem is to fix the socket at a distance of two to four feet from your plants. Naturally, the farther removed from the plants, the less effective is the light supply. The correct approach is to employ a method that produces maximum spectrum; minimum, non-required heat; and considerable light intensity.

The minimum requirement of one thousand foot-candle power at the source can be achieved by using four 40 watt tubes that are forty-eight inches long. If you decide to use a twenty-four inch length, you will still need four tubes; they are now reduced to 20 watts, and the intensity of the light is reduced although not proportionately.

One fixture that is currently being tested may be another solution to the problem of lighting for indoor vegetable growing. It is a very high-output fixture using 110 watt *Power Groove* fluorescent tubes. These are still Cool White tubes that lack some of the red spectrum, but this may be overcome by using two or three 15 watt incandescent bulbs. Two main questions that are presently being probed are whether the

increased intensity compensates for the lack of red in this arrangement
and whether there is too much heat generated by the *Power Groove*.
Excessive heat, of course, could cause crop burn, especially if the 15
watt bulbs are used to round out the spectrum.

The temperature under your lights is of singular importance regardless of light intensity. Should the leaf temperature go above 85° F
(29°C), the plant can no longer carry out photosynthesis to any great
extent. Remember that leaf temperature can be considerably higher
than room temperature. In this situation, a crucial part could be played
by a small fan placed near the growing area to circulate air and keep the
temperature within acceptable limits. Don't point the fan right at the
plants.

The *Power Groove* tubes have over 2000 foot-candle power. This
is the first time that anything over approximately 1200 foot-candle
power has been available from fluorescents. In addition to expense, the
problems of spectrum and temperature still must be solved to make the
use of such high-output fixtures suitable for the indoor gardener.

On the cheaper side of the spectrum, it is possible to use Cool
White tubes. As mentioned, the addition of two small incandescent
bulbs of 15 watts each will help make up for the deficiency of red in these
tubes. The materials to ask for are:

1. Four medium, bi-pin, rapid start Cool White tubes
2. Two 15 watt refrigerator bulbs. (These are smaller than a
   standard 15 watt bulb, lessening the danger of direct contact
   with foliage.)
3. A mount, preferably with a hood, to hold these items.

Another combination that works well is two Warm White and two
Cool White tubes. As seen by the table below, deficiencies of spectrum
can be kept to a minimum when tubes are used in combination.

RELATIVE LIGHT EMISSION QUANTITIES OF WHITE FLUORESCENT LAMPS

Name	Violet-Blue Required by Plants	Orange-Red Required by Plants
Cool White	good	good
Day Light	excellent	deficient
Warm White	deficient	very good
Natural White	deficient	excellent

If you are going to invest in the more expensive category of grow-tubes, it is worthwhile to get the best. In my opinion, this is the *Duro-Test Vita-Lite* medium, bi-pin rapid start tube. No extra tubes are necessary when using such a fixture, because four of these tubes produce enough red by themselves.

These recommendations don't discount the fact that there are mixed views by the experts on what is the best light source for indoor vegetable growing. Part of the reason for these divergent views is that nothing yet devised by man is able to totally replace the sun, which provides us with eight to ten thousand foot-candle power on a bright day. Everything we use for indoor hydroponics is at best a poor second.

When setting up your own or buying a lighting system for your indoor garden, don't forget that most plant fixtures use only two fluorescent tubes, just enough for ornamental plants, but often insufficient for vegetables, some herbs and flowers. Your hydroponic system will need four tubes and at least one thousand foot-candle power illumination at the source. Even with the four tubes, depending on their kind, of course, power consumption can be kept as low as 190 watts, no more than a table lamp.

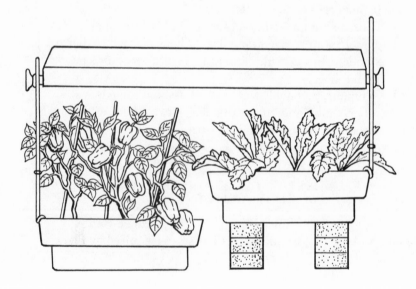

Figure 13. Tall and short plants can be grown under the same light by raising the planter of small plants with bricks or blocks.

PRACTICAL USE OF LIGHTING

Keep the light low over the plants. Two to four inches is reasonable. Vegetables, flowers and herbs need much stronger light than ordinary house plants. If they don't get it, they will grow weak, spindly and pale.

Raise the light source whenever the growing plants touch the tubes or bulbs. Two feet is the highest it should be raised; otherwise the lower plants won't get enough light.

Illuminate your plants sixteen to eighteen hours a day. An occasional night with the lights on is less harmful than a day with them off. To make things easier, plug the light into an automatic, heavy-duty, grounded timer — the kind that accepts a three-pronged plug.

SOME LIGHT LEVEL REQUIREMENTS

Very High	High	Medium	
Eggplant	Bean	Beet	Mustard
Pepper	Cantaloupe	Brussels sprouts	Parsley
Tomato	Corn	Cabbage	Parsnip
	Cucumber	Carrot	Pea
	Okra	Cauliflower	Radish
	Spanish onion	Celery	Spinach
	Squash	Chive	Spring onion
	Zucchini	Kale	Swiss chard
		Kohlrabi	Turnip (medium
		Leek	to high)
		Lettuce	

Temperature

Indoors or outdoors, vegetables grow best within a definite temperature range of 55°F (13°C) to 85°F (29°C). Indoors, you are striving for an average range of 72°F (22°C) during the day and 62-65°F (16-18°C) at night. Plants need this day and night variance, for during the day they manufacture energy and at night they assimilate it and grow. Without a definite temperature variation, the plants will receive confusing signals and attempt to continue producing energy continuously.

Temperature is also linked to the rate of photosynthesis. Plants can live, but they cease to grow as the temperature approaches the freezing point. Temperate zone plants have an upper limit of about 85-90°F (29-32°C). Above this level, functions such as flower growth can be reversed. Tropical zone plants, on the other hand, have a higher tolerance through natural adaptation.

If you are growing indoors during the summer, air conditioning might be a good idea, because high, oppressive heat without good air circulation can cause excessive transpiration and wilting. However, air conditioning may result in humidity problems, so you may have to do a little experimenting to strike the right combination. If you do use an air conditioner, it is better to either run it all the time, or only at night; otherwise you may unwittingly be sending scrambled signals to your plants. Of course, my own recommendation is to move your hydroponic garden outside for the summer where you will be taking advantage of natural (and free) sunlight without the bother of temperature and light problems.

The winter is another story altogether. Many people live in a winter environment where the temperature is constantly changing. This could occur, for example, in an old three or four storey apartment building that is heated with hot water radiators. The superintendent stokes up the boiler and everyone swelters; the radiators cool down and everyone freezes. The individual tenant has little or no control over the consistency of heat, short of opening a window or turning on the stove. Under such conditions, careful consideration and planning must be given to temperature control. Turning your growing lights off every evening for six to eight hours will provide some of the required temperature drop but not more than about 5°F (3°C).

Plants dislike drafts, so consideration must be given to where your plants are placed relative to doors and windows during the winter. Your hydroponic tanks should not be placed over forced air vents or radiators. The high temperature blasts that occur in such situations can convey confusing signals to the plants, because one area is very warm while another is considerably cooler. These high temperatures can also cause excessive transpiration and dehydration. The eventual results of these problems, if uncorrected, can be uneven growth, dropping of leaves and perhaps an end to growth.

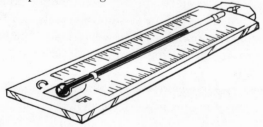

Humidity

Humidity plays an important role in hydroponics, but if you are growing in a house or apartment, you will find that this is the one aspect of climate over which you have relatively little control unless you have a humidifier-dehumidifier. Too much humidity will probably be less of a problem than too little humidity. If your growing area is too dry, you could install an inexpensive humidifier. Because the growing area is usually small and confined, greenhouse hydroponics for the hobbyist makes humidity easier to adjust, although it may be expensive.

Do keep in mind, however, that a hydroponic system in your home is a wonderful, natural humidifier during the winter. In most North American homes, the air is far too dry, leading to various respiratory problems and colds. A hydroponic system provides humidity in two ways: through evaporation of the water in the nutrient solution, and through plant transpiration. This is yet another area where hydroponics gives Mother Nature a helping hand.

Anything can be taken beyond reasonable limits, though, and I can remember a few years ago having sixteen tanks in an enclosed, ten by ten foot room. Needless to say, the room was soon like a rain forest! I ended up installing an air conditioner to pull some of the moisture out. It is important to remember that plants need some humidity, especially during germination, but that a balance needs to be struck between the rain forest and the desert.

The pollination period is also affected by humidity. As mentioned in Chapter 2, growing indoors makes it necessary for you to do your own pollinating, and if the humidity is too high or too low this process becomes more difficult. The whole question of pollination will be covered in Chapter 10.

Indoors, lighting affects temperature, while temperature and humidity go hand in hand. An ideal temperature-humidity combination for vegetables is 40 per cent relative humidity at 70°F (21°C). This simply means that 40 per cent of the atmosphere is moisture vapour at that temperature. Because warm air is capable of carrying a greater proportion of moisture than cold air before it precipitates (rain, fog), the 40 per cent figure at 70°F means a greater amount of moisture is present than at 65°F (18°C) with the same humidity reading.

Plants prefer relatively high humidity. If the air around them is too dry, they will transpire more in an effort to increase the amount of moisture in the air. In effect, low humidity could make the plants exhaust themselves. When people perspire, they need to replace the lost body fluids or they risk dehydration. Plants must also be able to absorb high amounts of water under low humidity conditions to keep up with the rate of transpiration. Often they are unable to do so, and the plants wilt. Tropical vegetables and fruits, such as cantaloupe and cucumber, like an even higher humidity level than most other plants. A good idea during the intense heat of a summer afternoon is to mist your plants two or three times. This will lessen the need for water through the root system and also reduce the rate of transpiration.

Because our indoor living environments are frequently very dry, it would be a good idea to purchase an inexpensive humidity measuring device and give high priority to both humidity and temperature. High humidity is not nearly as much of a problem for two reasons: first, it is unlikely that you will be able to create such a situation in your home, and second, plants can cope with a high reading, but not its opposite. The only possible problems that could be caused by too high a humidity are the development of mold or mildew and, as mentioned earlier, the effect it could have on pollination.

When using your hydroponic unit indoors, make sure you establish a definite daily temperature variance with warmer days and cooler nights. There are energy saving thermostats on the market that do this automatically. In fact, I should point out that plants, like children, love a routine. The daytime temperature, nighttime temperature and the periods of having your lights on and off should always be as consistent as possible.

Here are the temperature preferences of the most common hydro-ponically grown vegetables. Keep in mind that 40 per cent humidity at 70°F (21°C) is your base figure for measuring the environment.

Cool: 50 to 70°F (10 to 20°C)		Warm: 60 to 80°F (16 to 26°C)	
Beet	Leek	Bean	Squash
Broccoli	Lettuce	Chinese cabbage	Tomato
Brussels sprouts	Onion	Corn	
Cabbage	Pea	Cucumber	
Cauliflower	Radish	Eggplant	
Celery	Spinach	Melon	
Chive	Watercress	Okra	
Kohlrabi		Pepper	

Remember, too, that an indoor atmosphere often contains dust and smoke. Regular spraying with water, about once a week, will clean plant pores and wash off dirt accumulations. Although such plants as cantaloupe, cucumber and zucchini like high humidity readings, they are not fond of excessive amounts of water on their leaves. Washing may cause a mildew infection on the leaves.

CHAPTER 6

Starting Up: Seeds, Transplants and Cuttings

For many people, a great deal of satisfaction will be gained from building a hydroponic system. For others, the interest and delight will centre around the actual planting and growing. Both groups are interested in good harvests. This chapter deals with starting up your system, whether built or bought, using seeds, transplants and cuttings.

In hydroponics, anything will grow: exotics — coconut palms, vanilla, ginger and nutmeg; houseplants — roses, carnations and zinnias; as well as edible plants — tomatoes, celery and basil. The choice is yours, and the only limitation is the depth of the medium for some root vegetables. You can grow flowers for cutting, house plants for decoration, or, best of all, vegetables and herbs to improve your meals.

When choosing vegetables to grow, you'll want to begin with those that taste best fresh and taste worst from the supermarket: tomatoes, lettuce, green peppers, wax beans, etc. Other vegetables, such as potatoes, carrots and turnips, don't suffer too much from long storage and are still worth buying from the corner chain store. So if you don't have any specific preferences start with tomatoes, lettuce, celery and spring onions, with a few herbs thrown in. Chapters 7 and 8 take a close look at raising edible plants: the information given in this chapter will hold for almost any plant.

Selecting Your Seeds

Be sure to ask for seed varieties especially suited for home growing. Commercial seed varieties have been bred for toughness and long shelf life in the supermarket at the expense of fragrance and flavour. You can plant more fragile, and more tasty, vegetable and herb varieties in your hydroponic garden.

Because very few seeds have been developed specifically for hydroponics, there are some hints to keep in mind. As an indoor home grower, you are better off with a bush or patio tomato, rather than a vine type, because of the unwieldy height the vines may grow to. Self-pollinating cucumbers are the easiest to use indoors, but if you take your garden outdoors, the self-pollinating cukes will be pollinated by insects and grow deformed. Leaf lettuce will yield a high volume of leaves in a few weeks, while head lettuce takes a bit longer. If you decide to use head lettuce, why not treat it as leaf lettuce and simply pick the leaves fresh for your salads. *Boston* and *Buttercrunch* are two popular varieties. Other than these general considerations, go ahead and use any seed that interests you.

Figure 14. Your spice rack is a fascinating source of seeds.

Besides obtaining seeds from garden centres and hardware stores, there are other, more interesting ways of getting them. Your spice rack is a fascinating source of seeds: coriander, caraway, mustard (great salad greens, by the way), celery, pepper, chili, fennel, dill and anise. From your pantry you can plant dried beans, lentils, chick peas, plain peas (not the split kind), and so on. Your table is another good source. If you like the taste of a cucumber, squash, tomato or melon, save the seeds and plant them with the pulp still clinging to them – that way they'll germinate even faster than dried seeds. It won't always work, because the seeds may have come from sterile hybrids, but it's fun to try.

You might also want to let your healthiest plants go to seed and use them for your next planting. Sometimes this gives superb results, but when hybrids are involved, it may not always be successful.

Seeding

You can plant seeds directly into your hydroponic garden, although the cautions concerning the flood and drain system mentioned earlier should be kept in mind. With a flood system it would be better to seed in jiffy pots, and at the right stage of development place the plant, jiffy pot and all, in your growing medium. In order to keep your main unit functioning at full capacity, you might wish to build or buy a smaller "nursery" tank. Raising seedlings in this way makes it possible to locate your plants precisely where you want them and to replace harvested plants with already grown seedlings raring to go.

Plant your seeds closer together than indicated on store-bought packages. The roots of hydroponic plants don't have to compete with each other for nutrient and much closer spacing is possible. You can

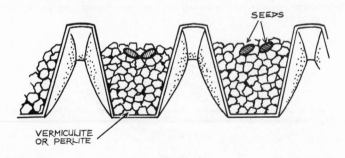

Figure 15. Tuck your seeds into the growing medium no deeper than one-half inch.

soak the seeds overnight in water for faster germination. Plant two seeds wherever you want to end up with one plant. If both come up, snip off the smaller one with scissors. Tuck your seeds into the growing medium no deeper than one or two pebbles or one-half inch.

Most seeds germinate best in darkness, warmth and moisture. These conditions may be created by covering your seeds with dark plastic film (a piece of heavy, green garbage bag will do). For those seeds that germinate best in light, use clear plastic. (See Herb Planting Guide, p. 86.) In windy locations, keep the germination covers from blowing away by placing a few pieces of growing medium on top.

Check every day (religiously!) under the covers for results. As soon as the first sprouts poke through the medium, take the covers off and let the light and air get at the seedlings. Failure to remove the covers soon enough will cause the seedlings to bolt. That is, they will grow long and spindly trying to get out from under the covers. If that happens, you may as well pull them out and start over. When part of a seeded planter has sprouted and part hasn't, cut or fold the covers as needed. Some seeds come up fast (basil, cucumbers), others are quite slow (parsley, peppers), so don't give up.

Identify what you have seeded with plant markers. Use a water-proof felt pen or pencil so that the writing won't wash off. If your seeds don't sprout, there are five possible reasons:

1. The seed bed is too cold for them (less than 56°F or 13°C)
2. You have bought old seed that is no longer fertile. (See Chapter 12 for seed storage.)
3. Your seeds were not treated for fungus resistance and have been eaten by fungus (fuzz on the kernels you dig up)
4. You've put your seeds under their germination covers, placed them in the bright, hot sun and cooked them. (Always keep a newly seeded garden out of direct summer sunlight.)
5. The seeds have come from sterile hybrids.

Transplants

When transplanting into a hydroponic garden, you'll notice some amazing facts. First, the transplanted plants keep right on growing without any shock, wilting or drooping. Second, you can successfully transplant not only small seedlings, but even fully grown plants as long as you do not damage their roots.

An ordinary egg carton will serve as a homemade nursery for raising seedlings to transplant. Any egg box will do, but the waterproof, plastic type is best. This will start you off with as many as twelve tomato plants, or any other type of seedling you wish to raise. If you use vermiculite or perlite as the growing medium in your nursery, the amount that clings to the roots when you transplant will not harm the effectiveness of the medium in your main unit. Don't be afraid to insert both the root system and the stem of your transplant up to the first set of leaves into the growing medium. The stem will develop root hairs, and a stronger plant will result.

Transplants that come from soil have to have their roots washed gently but *completely* to remove any dirt clinging to them. Use cold water, running steadily from the tap. The water will help to loosen the

Figure 16. Before transplanting a soil-grown plant into a hydroponic garden, gently wash its roots under cold water to remove any dirt clinging to them.

soil, while its coldness has an anaesthetizing effect on the plant. By the time the transplant "comes to," it is already growing in its new environment and is unlikely to go into shock. You will probably have less success transplanting vegetables from soil than you will the hardier herbs or house plants.

Some shock will be apparent when transplanting flowering house plants like African Violets from soil. The plant will probably lose all its flowers, and it might even wilt considerably. Don't despair. There is an excellent chance that the plant will survive, and in five to six days you will see it perk up. Then the plant will likely go through a new flowering cycle and give you some of the best blooms you have ever seen.

No washing is, of course, necessary with hydroponically raised transplants. For both methods, though, the byword is *be gentle with the roots.*

To transplant, simply make a hole in the growing medium down through the drainage medium if you are using one. Drop the roots in and close the growing medium around them. Do not try to untangle the roots from vermiculite or perlite used in a nursery. With soil transplants, try to spread the clean, exposed roots around a little.

Cuttings

Any plants that will successfully root from cuttings can be placed directly into your soilless garden. Clean the leaves from the last two inches of stem, and, if possible, coat the stem with a root hormone. This procedure is not as useful with vegetables as it is with some herbs and decorative plants. Still, it is not only fun, but free, to collect a few cuttings from your friends. The possibilities are endless. For example, one good trick with tomatoes is to let a few suckers grow on a plant until they are three or four inches long, cut them off at the base and stick them deeply into your growing medium. That way, you'll have more tomato plants.

Although seeds can be placed closer together in hydroponics than they can in soil, don't forget that different plants require different amounts of room to spread their leaves and fruit. In the next chapters we will look at specific plant varieties and discuss the amount of room each requires in a hydroponic garden.

CHAPTER 7

Hydroponic Vegetables

Almost any plant or vegetable will grow hydroponically. The questions you have to ask yourself are: why do you want to grow it? What is your purpose for having a hydroponic garden? How large is your unit? How many units do you have?

If you are planning to use your soilless garden for a hobby or to pass the time, go ahead and have fun. Plant whatever interests you, and don't be afraid to experiment. The level of knowledge of hydroponics today is about the same as that in mathematics two hundred years ago. We have much to learn about the subject, and you can help. Even the experts are constantly learning and experimenting. In my opinion, the only criterion is to have fun. Try everything.

For those who are really serious about the crops they want to harvest, my advice is to stick mostly to salad vegetables. Through hybridization, it is mainly the salad vegetables that commercial growers have altered until much of their original nutritional value and flavour have been lost. Plastic lettuce, swampy tomatoes, soggy radishes and hollow celery are only a few examples.

Of course, you will be limited by the amount of space, time and money you have to devote to the whole idea. Practical considerations should come into play here. For example, six tomato vines, each producing six pounds of tomatoes from a sixteen by twenty-four inch container is a more efficient use of space than sixteen stalks of corn.

The following instructions are given to help the home hydroponic vegetable grower. (A few fruits that can be grown hydroponically have also been included.) Information given on nutrient requirements will be helpful for those people who are making their own. There are a few general points to keep in mind. When several species of vegetables are grown in one tank and a commercial nutrient is used, care must be taken not to upset the balance. Also remember, when seeding or transplanting into your soilless garden, that the entire area can be utilized for growing and the limitation on how far apart to place your seeds is conditional upon the physical air space the plant requires to grow. For example, a pea vine climbing up a string requires far less air space than a bushy tomato vine.

BEANS

Beans will grow winter or summer, indoors or out. In winter, grow bush beans indoors. In summer, grow pole beans outdoors. Pole varieties can be tied up and grown vertically. They can be planted quite close together (about six inches). As their name implies, bush beans tend to take up more room. Beans require less nitrogen than other crops but need large amounts of phosphorus, potassium and sulphur. Limas do not produce as large a crop, and they take longer to mature.

BEETS

Root vegetables are best grown in vermiculite with relatively little soaking. Only a slight covering of haydite or gravel should be used to minimize algae buildup. Most varieties of beets do well. They like cool temperatures. Plant about three inches apart. Grow smaller beets, and more of them, for greater tenderness.

BROCCOLI

Several experts claim that this is a good crop. I have not grown many, because it is not a personal favourite. Transplants should be used, spaced seven inches apart. Broccoli likes cool weather (60°F, 16°C). Large amounts of nitrogen, phosphorus and iron can be important.

CABBAGE

I have grown cabbage without letting it head. As you would for leaf lettuce, pick the leaves for dinner and let it keep on growing. Plant six inches apart. Cabbage requires cool weather and high levels of nitrogen, phosphorus and iron.

CARROTS

Gourmet carrots are better to grow than the common varieties because of the depth of the growing medium. Plant about one and a half inches apart. Potassium and phosphorus are important.

CAULIFLOWER

I have had bad luck with cauliflower for good reasons. It is very susceptible to temperature variations. If you are growing cauliflower with other crops, it is better to grow it with plants having moderately cool requirements. Plant about eight inches apart. Nitrogen, phosphorus and iron are required in larger amounts.

CELERY

This is a great salad vegetable to grow. Celery does best on the cool side, and it dislikes temperature extremes. Plant about four inches apart and use the young stalks and leaves for your salad. It is best about two months old and pencil thin. By the time it is four months old, it is useful only for soups and stews. Don't uproot an entire plant; simply cut off a few stalks at a time. Larger amounts of sodium and chlorine are usually important.

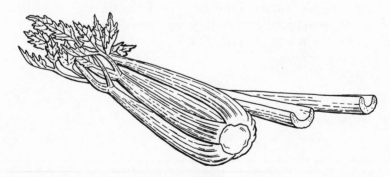

CHARD

This is a good crop that can be harvested much like head lettuce. Keep removing the outer leaves for your meals. Plant four inches apart and keep cool. Chard is fantastic cooked like spinach.

CORN

Corn is a possible crop, but it is not popular, because of the small harvest. Plant midget corn about six inches apart.

CUCUMBERS

Along with lettuce and tomatoes, this is a popular commercial crop. If you don't wish to cross-pollinate (see Chapter 10), plant the English or seedless variety. These grow well indoors or in greenhouses, but if you grow them outdoors and insects do the pollinating, you may end up with some unusually shaped cukes. They like hot weather and direct sunlight and are sometimes susceptible to mildew.

EGGPLANT

This is a possible but not a popular crop. Eggplants are slow germinators and like warm weather. They will grow larger if you pinch some of the flowers off, allowing only a few fruit per vine. Extra amounts of nitrogen, phosphorus and potassium are required, but reduce the nitrogen, if possible, after the fruit has formed.

LEEK

You'll get a good crop by adding increased amounts of nitrogen and potassium and extra amounts of phosphorus.

LETTUCE

Boston and New York are popular heading varieties, but leaf lettuce yields a larger harvest. If you do grow head lettuce, remove the outer leaves for salads without waiting for it to head and you can increase your crop. Grand Rapids and Salad Bowl are great leaf lettuce, but don't forget Romaine (Romagna) for Caesar Salad.

In six weeks or less you can have an abundance of lettuce. However, caution should be exercised during the first two weeks. Lettuce will bolt (small leaves will grow on a long, stringy stem) with insufficient light or high temperatures. Varieties that don't bolt as frequently are *Black-Seeded Simpson, Endive, Escarolle* and *Batavia.* It would be a good idea to cut back on your nutrient a bit for this crop. Lettuce likes it cool (50-70°F, 10-21°C) with high nitrogen levels. Plant about four inches apart, close to the edges of your planter so that the heads hang over them.

MELONS

The growing techniques for melons are similar to those for cucumbers. They like to be warm both day and night. High humidity causes mildew, so keep them well ventilated. *Honey Dew* is a good cantaloupe, and if you want to try watermelon, get an early variety such as *Sugar Baby*. Remember to cross-pollinate. Tie up the vines, and when growing indoors, provide plenty of light.

ONIONS

Spring Onions or *Green Bunching* are popular. They should be sown rather heavily, one-half inch apart. Requires larger amounts of potassium and nitrogen.

PEAS

All varieties do well in hydroponics, but try *Snow Peas* with their sweet and flavourful edible pods. Use a lot of plants to get several good meals. Tie them up or let them grow up a trellis. Plant three inches apart and maintain cool temperatures.

PEPPERS

All peppers are great to grow: *Green Bell, Yellow Banana* or *Chili.* Grow
them together or separately. Peppers are fond of warm weather. Plant
them six inches apart and watch for damping off. Peppers are harder to
grow indoors than out because they need high light levels that are not
always obtainable with indoor lighting. My experience is that peppers
and tomatoes don't like each other. I haven't met anyone or read any
book that makes this claim, yet when I have the two side by side
indoors, the tomatoes stop growing. (A list of "friends" and "enemies"
will be found under the heading Companion Planting at the end of this
chapter.)

RADISHES

Most varieties are suitable, but as with beets, it is better to grow them in
vermiculite and plant about one and one-half inches apart. Keep the
vermiculite about half as moist as you normally would. Radishes bolt
very easily, so make sure they have ample light and cool temperatures.
Water only should be used for the first two or three weeks when radishes
are being grown by themselves. Normally, radishes are grown in the
worst part of a soil garden, but in hydroponics, they have the best of
everything, and if you aren't careful you will get a lot of tops before the
root has a chance to grow.

SPINACH

Spinach can be a fast crop. Plant two to three inches apart. Cool
temperatures and plenty of nitrogen are needed.

SQUASH AND ZUCCHINI

These are grown in basically the same way as cucumbers, but remember how much space a zucchini occupies and plant eight to nine inches apart. Pinch the plant off after six or seven sets of leaves to keep the energy closer to the root system and to ensure fruiting.

STRAWBERRIES

These are good for hydroponics, but not very economical unless you are intercropping (see page 76). Try to get a self-pollinating variety like *Ozark Beauty*. Plant them eight inches apart and sit back for a long time. Strawberry plants, like asparagus, need two to three years to mature.

TOMATOES

Although the tomato is really a fruit, it is commonly counted among the vegetables. This is one of the best and most satisfying hydroponic crops. Indoors you should seed bush or patio tomatoes, so that the plants will stay nicely under your lights. Outdoors you could grow staking tomatoes but the bush variety is still easier to work with in hydroponics, especially if the vines have not yet finished producing when you are ready to bring them in at the end of the summer.

Seed tomatoes for the early and late outdoor crop as shown here. Use a similar seeding pattern even if you use less than half of a planter. Plant the seeds for your early tomato crop in February or March indoors under lights and move them outdoors in April or May. Fan out the plants on your balcony or patio using strings or trellises as shown on page 110.

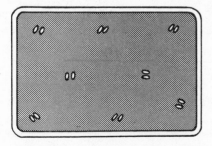 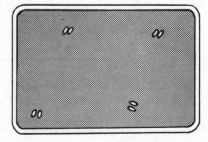

Figure 17. Seed tomatoes for the early and late outdoor crops as shown on the left. For your winter crop, grown indoors, plant the seeds as shown on the right.

OTHER VEGETABLES

There are many other vegetables you might want to plant. If you are not familiar with their growing, read one of the many books on home gardening. Herbs are covered in the next chapter.

Basically, you can grow anything outdoors, regardless of how far its vines may spread. Indoors you can only grow what you can illuminate, and you are better off sticking to bush, dwarf or patio varieties that will stay under your lights. Other types of plants will have to be pruned when they grow tall or when their vines range too far. I recommend that you concentrate indoors on such crops as lettuce, tomatoes, other salad vegetables and herbs — all items that provide nutrition at a time when it is most needed and most expensive from the supermarket.

Outdoors it makes sense to use the available hydroponic growing area to its fullest. This may be done by intercropping and outcropping. Intercropping means combining two or more different plants in space and time. That is, you can place short plants at the base of tall ones and

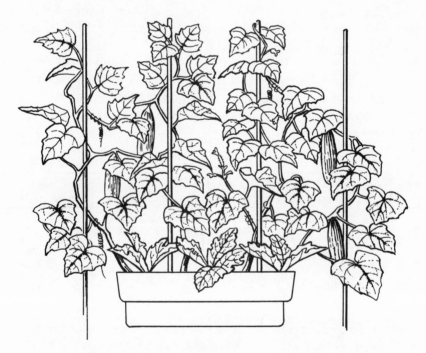

Figure 18. Intercropping lettuce and cucumbers.

fast growing plants between slower types. A fast growing crop, such as radishes or leaf lettuce, will have come up and been harvested by the time the space is needed for a slower crop.

Outcropping means letting your plants spread out from the planter, up, down and sideways. The layout shown here gives you an idea of how to obtain growth and yield far greater than the available growing area seems to permit.

A few reminders are in order. If you want to grow root vegetables, like carrots and radishes, there are two things to keep in mind. First, irrigate them for the first week or two after planting with plain water only, until they have established themselves as short, stocky plants. Only then add nutrient to the water. Second, you shouldn't grow anything with a root much longer than three inches because of the relatively shallow depth of the medium. This is not a problem with round radishes, only the icicle variety, and there are short, barrel-shaped carrot varieties on the seed shelf too.

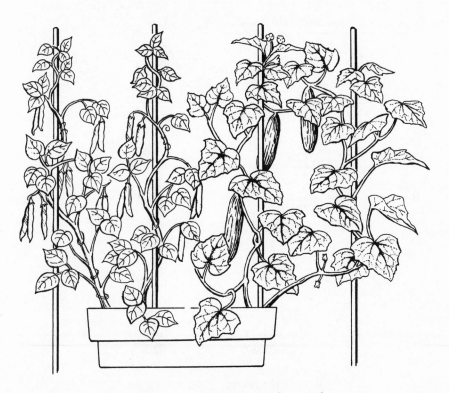

Figure 19. Outcropping beans and cucumbers.

Companion Planting

Plants don't make a sound, and you'd think that their world was all peace and harmony. Not so – among plants there are definite friends and enemies. Some plants protect each other from insect infestations, while others provide shade for their friends. Still others just like each other and grow better if they are neighbours. In hydroponics, you will probably be asking two or more plants to grow happily together. Here is the list. Keep the friends and enemies apart.

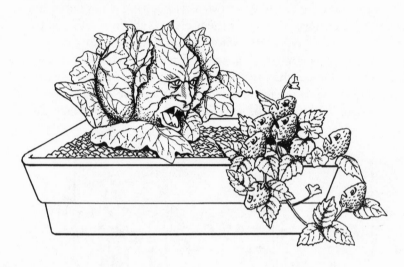

Plant	Friends	Enemies
anise	coriander	–
asparagus	basil	–
	parsley	
	tomato	
basil, sweet	asparagus	rue
bean, bush	beet	fennel
	cabbage	garlic
	carrot	onion
	cauliflower	rue
	cucumber	shallot
	potato	
	summer savory	
	strawberry	

Plant	Friends	Enemies
bean, pole	carrot	beet
	cauliflower	fennel
	corn, sweet	garlic
	cucumber	kohlrabi
	radish	onion
	savory	shallot
beet	bean, bush	bean, pole
	cabbage	
	chive	
	kohlrabi	
	lettuce	
	onion	
	shallot	
borage	strawberry	~
broccoli	cabbage	~
	tomato	
Brussels sprouts	tomato	~
cabbage	bean, bush	bean, pole
	beet	strawberry
	broccoli	tomato
	camomile	
	celery	
	dill	
	lettuce	
	mint	
	potato	
	sage	
camomile	cabbage	~
caraway	~	fennel
carrot	bean, bush	dill
	bean, pole	
	chive	
	leek	
	lettuce	
	onion	
	pea rosemary	
	potato sage	
	radish tomato	

Plant	Friends	Enemies
cauliflower	bean, bush bean, pole tomato	~
celeriac	bean, bush cauliflower cabbage leek tomato	~
celery	bean, bush cabbage cauliflower leek tomato	~
chervil	radish	~
chives	beet carrot	bean pea
coriander	anise	fennel
corn, sweet	bean, bush bean, pole cucumber pea potato pumpkin squash	~
cucumber	bean, bush bean, pole pea radish sunflower	aromatic herbs potato sage
dill	cabbage	carrot tomato
fennel	~	bean, bush bean, pole caraway coriander kohlrabi tomato

Plant	Friends	Enemies
garlic	beet	bean, bush
	onion	bean, pole
		pea
grape	hyssop	~
hyssop	grape	radish
kale	tomato	~
kohlrabi	beet	bean, pole
	onion	fennel
		tomato
leek	carrot	~
	celeriac	
	celery	
	onion	
lettuce	beet	~
	cabbage	
	carrot	
	cucumber	
	onion	
	radish	
	strawberry	
onion	beet	bean, bush
	carrot	bean, pole
	garlic	pea
	kohlrabi	
	lettuce	
	savory	
	strawberry	
	tomato	
parsley	asparagus	~
	tomato	
pea	bean	garlic
	carrot	onion
	corn, sweet	shallot
	cucumber	
	potato	
	radish	
	turnip	

Plant	Friends	Enemies
pumpkin	corn, sweet	potato
radish	bean, pole	hyssop
	carrot	
	chervil	
	cucumber	
	lettuce	
	nasturtium	
	pea	
rosemary	sage	~
rue	~	sweet basil
sage	cabbage	cucumber
	rosemary	
summer savory	bean, bush	~
shallot	beet	bean, bush
		bean, pole
		pea
spinach	strawberry	~
squash	corn	~
	nasturtium	
strawberry	bean, bush	cabbage
	borage	
	lettuce	
	onion	
	spinach	
sunflower	cucumber	potato
tomato	asparagus	cabbage
	carrot	dill
	chive	fennel
	kale	kohlrabi
	marigold	
	nasturtium	
	nettle, stinging	
	onion	
	parsley	
turnip	pea	~

Garden Flowers and House Plants

This chapter has concentrated on vegetables and the next will centre on herbs. But let's not forget flowers and house plants. Anything that blossoms in a dirt garden or flower pot will do even better in a hydroponic planter, summer or winter, from asters to zinnias. The same holds true for house plants. They are children of the tropics and survive in our latitudes mostly in a state of permanent hibernation. Both seeds and transplants do extremely well in hydroponics, and it is amazing to watch them grow in a fertile environment in much the same way as they would in the tropics. House plants use much less water than vegetables or flowers, but because of the excellent aeration properties of a hydroponic medium your plants can never be overwatered. This is the most common cause of death among potted house plants. Again, keep friends and enemies apart. Consult a companion planting guide book specifically for flower and house plants. When seeding flowers, you are probably better off with varieties that grow up to 9 or 12 inches because in hydroponics they will grow twice as high. Flowers that grow over 12 inches in soil gardens will be too unwieldy grown hydroponically.

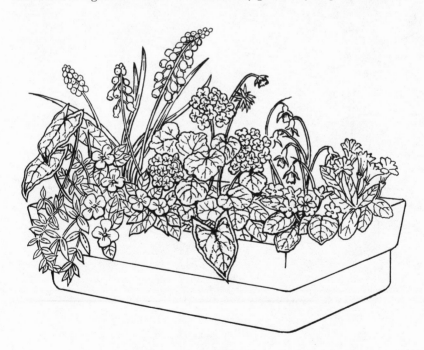

CHAPTER 8

Fresh Herbs

In our unthinking acceptance of highly processed convenience foods, we have almost forgotten those magical plants that have served mankind for thousands of years by pleasing the sense of smell, helping the digestion and lending their special flavours to food. Commercial chemists are still trying in vain to match these tastes and aromas. The expensive dried herbs that can be bought at the supermarket in fancy little bottles are only a pale echo of the real thing. Most of the vitamins, fragrance and flavour have been lost in processing and exposure to air.

In a hydroponic garden, it is possible to raise all kinds of herbs. These can be included in a large system that supports other plants, as long as friends and enemies are kept apart, or you can raise them separately in a smaller herb garden. Lights aren't always necessary for indoor growing. A sunny window with a southern or western exposure should make it possible to grow satisfactory crops. Not only that, but a small kitchen garden full of colourful and fragrant herbs is a charming addition to any cooking area. Outdoors, of course, herbs thrive.

The most important herbs for cooking are: basil, chive, chervil, dill, lovage, marjoram, oregano, parsley (curly or plain), sage, savory, tarragon and thyme. There are many others you might want to try, and for obtaining more exotic seeds, see the Resource List at the end of this book. Just remember, for seeding indoors and out, don't put more than four or five different herbs in a single planter or they get too crowded. Always plant two seeds per location and thin out the losers. Don't throw them away; save them, stems and all, for soups or salads. When planning the layout of your kitchen garden, place the tall herbs in the rear and the lower ones in the front to make harvesting easier.

Some herbs, tarragon for example, have a very poor germination rate. You would be wise to plant four or five seeds where you want only one plant. Other kinds, like parsley, are slow to sprout. For these herbs, you may want to start up more quickly with transplants or cuttings. Because of its tall and narrow "leaves," chive can be seeded close together, almost as you would sow grass seed. Most herbs, such as basil and sage, germinate very quickly.

The information given below will help you germinate and harvest your herbs. The growing time to the first cut you make in the Herb Yields chart includes the germinating time shown in the Planting Guide. All of these plants can last from four to eight months before they need replanting. Some can last as long as twelve months, if the plants and unit are kept clean.

HERB PLANTING GUIDE

Dark Covers	Clear Covers	Days for Germinating
Anise		7-10
	Basil	2-4
Borage		3-5
	Camomile	2-4
Chervil		4-7
Chive		7-10
Coriander		5-7
Dill		3-5
Fennel		4-7
	Lemon Balm	7-14
Marjoram		3-5
	Mint	10-14
	Mustard	2-4
Onion		2-5
Oregano		3-5
Parsley		5-7
Rosemary		4-7
Sage		4-7
	Savory	6-10
	Sorrel	2-5
Tarragon		7-10
Thyme		5-7
Watercress		3-5

HERB YIELDS

Variety	Growing Time		Yield (ounces)	
	1st Cut	Replacement	1st Cut	Replacement
Basil	9-14 days	4-7 days	9	15
Chervil	12-16	7	5	8
Chive	15-20	7-10	3	5-8
Coriander	15-20	7	5	8
Dill	12-15	5-7	5	8
Marjoram	12-15	5-7	4	5
Mint	24-30	7-10	6	10
Onion (seed)	10-15	7-10	5	7-10
Oregano	13-18	4-7	4	5
Parsley	13-18	7	5	8
Rosemary	15-24	10	6	8
Sage	12-18	6-9	8	12
Savory	14-20	7-10	8	12
Sorrel	14-19	7-10	8	12
Tarragon	20-30	10	5	8
Thyme	18-24	7-10	3	5
Watercress	12-15	6-10	5	8

This information was kindly supplied to me by Applied Hydroponics of Canada, Montreal.

If you've never tried cooking with fresh herbs, aside from parsley which seems to be about all we use these days, then you are in for a pleasant surprise. An indication of the startling difference between fresh and dry herbs can be gotten by doing a small test. Go to your spice rack and smell the contents of the jar of dried marjoram leaves, then crush a fresh leaf between your fingers and bring it to your nose. You should now be completely hooked on growing and using fresh herbs.

Cooking with fresh herbs needn't be confined to gourmet dishes; everyday meals will benefit greatly from their use, particularly with bland vegetables like potatoes and lima beans. Recipes will be provided in the next chapter for both kinds of dishes. To whet your appetite, though, remember that whatever kind of meal you are serving, hydroponics will make it possible to have a fresh green salad winter or summer.

BASIL

Basil has a special affinity for tomatoes. It is the secret that accounts for many delicious southern Italian dishes containing tomatoes, such as spaghetti and ravioli sauces. Northern Italy is famous for *pesto* butter, that lovely pasta cream made with fresh basil. This herb will lend a new and interesting flavour to practically all foods. It is one of the few herbs that actually increases in flavour when cooked. Try sprinkling fresh, chopped basil on a tomato salad.

CHERVIL

Chervil improves the flavour of any herb with which it is mixed, making it a constant ingredient in the *fines herbes* of French cooking. Chervil's mild flavour makes generous use necessary. Sprinkle it on peas, spinach, tomatoes and eggplant before serving. It tastes best if added to foods that don't need cooking. Using it in a soup or sauce means it should be added last and the dish should only be allowed to boil once more. For special occasions, use two or three good handfuls of fresh chervil in French chervil soup.

CHIVE

The smallest of the onion tribe, chive has a subtle flavour. It is one of the best culinary herbs, making fatty foods more digestible and giving a special piquancy to almost anything. In melted butter or sour cream, chive is the finishing touch to mashed, boiled or baked potatoes. It is excellent when used on salads, soups, in cottage cheese, devilled eggs or in the famous Green Sauce that will be given later. Chive can't be dried. Mind you, dried chive is being sold, but one taste of each kind will show what I mean. For breakfast, fold fresh, chopped chive into scrambled eggs halfway through the proceedings.

DILL

The lacy leaves of dill are delicately aromatic and when finely chopped yield a very special, sharp and

interesting flavour. There are three main uses for
dill: with fish (particularly in sauces), for flavouring
bland vegetables like peas and potatoes, and in seed
form for pickling cucumbers and cabbage. Try
sprinkling fresh, chopped dill on a cucumber salad.

Dill grows tall and graceful (two to three feet)
and other things can be planted beneath it. However, don't grow dill next to fennel; they cross-
pollinate and produce strange and useless offspring
that are neither dill nor fennel.

LOVAGE

This giant herb has a strong scent reminiscent of
yeast or the famous soup extract, Maggi. It gives
strength to soups, stews, casseroles, salads and
mixed vegetables. This extraordinary herb deserves
a bit of experimenting. Lovage is an important flavouring for some vegetarians, for it provides the
tastes normally associated with meat or soup bones.
For everyday use, put finely chopped lovage in or on
a soup. The aromatic seeds can also be used.

MARJORAM

Sweet marjoram has a milder and slightly different
flavour than its cousin, wild marjoram (oregano). It
is a meat herb and benefits pork, veal, lamb, poultry,
venison and sausages. Sweet marjoram is good in
such diverse foods as stuffings, omelets, Bloody
Marys and cottage cheese. Put fresh, chopped marjoram in your next poultry stuffing.

OREGANO

This herb is a favourite in Italian, Spanish and
Mexican dishes. Its hot flavour is best in tomato
dishes, spaghetti, pizza, hamburgers, meat loaf,
sauces, stews and stuffings. Tomato or bean soup is
much improved by the addition of a small quantity
of oregano. Oregano in cooking is as old as the
Greek hills where it originated, and it has both
stimulating and medicinal properties. For a flavourful dish, cook chopped, fresh oregano leaves in a
spaghetti sauce.

To make the plant spread, keep snipping the buds of the top leaf growth.

PARSLEY

Parsley underlines the taste of food. It has a remarkable gift for overcoming strong odours on the breath, even the powerful garlic is largely neutralized by it. In large amounts, it is a good natural tranquilizer. The finely chopped leaves are added twice in cooking; at the beginning when other flavours are brought out, and again shortly before serving. For everyday use, sprinkle chopped parsley on buttered, boiled new potatoes.

Parsley is a carefree crop, but very slow to germinate. An old tale claims that the seeds must go to the devil and back nine times before sprouting, so don't give up.

SAGE

The beautiful gray-green leaves of this wisest of all the mints is a must in every kitchen. The ancients thought it prolonged life, the Chinese love it as a tea for medicinal purposes and the modern family uses this incredibly fragrant herb on a modest scale in cheese dishes and sausages. With pork and fatty meats, sage is almost indispensable because it aids in digestion. Who would ever think of stuffing the Christmas turkey without using it? For everyday use, any stuffing will benefit from sage.

SAVORY

The traditional use of savory in bean dishes had its origin in making them easier to digest. Savory also gives its distinct and attractive flavour to stuffings, meat pies and sausages. Its fresh tops can be cooked with peas, lentils and beans of all kinds. Every kind of uncooked salad benefits from savory. A few leaves added to the water when cooking Brussels sprouts or cabbage improve their flavour and reduce cooking odour. For everyday use, cook fresh, chopped savory with lentils or broad beans.

TARRAGON

Tarragon is the king of all culinary herbs and has had
a most distinguished career, particularly in French
cuisine. It is used freely, chopped in salad dressings,
sprinkled over salads and main dishes such as steak
or fish, and on all vegetables. Melted butter with
chopped tarragon or tarragon sauces are excellent
company for delicate vegetables such as mushrooms,
eggplant or asparagus. Try tarragon in fish and poultry stuffings and in marinades. For everyday use, put
fresh, chopped tarragon in a sour cream salad
dressing.

    The best tarragon is the French or True tarra-
gon. It can only be raised by propagation. The
Russian tarragon that is found in seed packages is a
poor second to the French variety.

THYME

You would almost think thyme was the twin sister of
sage, since they go so well together. The beautiful,
broad, dark green leaves of the English variety and
the narrow gray-green leaves of the French type are
the most flavourful and popular of all thymes. In
early Greek and Roman days it was used on the body
as an antiseptic. Today, however, it is without equal
as an additive for soups, sauces and stuffing. Few
serious cooks would think of preparing pork, lamb or
chowder without a hint of thyme. Try some fresh,
chopped thyme on onion soup.

CHAPTER 9

Recipes Using Hydroponic Herbs

Most of the following recipes have been contributed by professional chefs who use hydroponic systems in their kitchens to grow their herbs. Some recipes are more difficult than others, but all are fun to try and delicious to eat. My thanks to these chefs for their willingness to share their expertise. It might be interesting to prepare one of these dishes yourself and, when in the chef's city, to try his version and compare the two. I have also included several of our own City Green recipes at the end of this chapter.

Michel Daublain
Chef Executif (Cours Culinaires), Le Château Frontenac, Quebec City

SAUCE VINCENT

1 ounce fresh parsley	*2 hard-boiled egg yolks*
1 ounce fresh watercress	*2 cups white mayonnaise*
2 ounces fresh spinach	*1 teaspoon Worcestershire sauce*

A combination of chervil, tarragon, chive, burnet and sorrel, to taste

Blanch and cool the vegetables and herbs, and press in a cloth to extract the water. Chop the two egg yolks and the vegetables and herbs together. Pass it all through a cheese cloth and mix with the mayonnaise and Worcestershire sauce. This sauce is excellent with a *saumon en belle-vue,* a *darne de saumon* or a *truite en gelée.*

DARNE DE SAUMON ~ SAUCE VINCENT

fish trimmings	*water*
1 *carrot*	*dry white wine*
1/2 *onion*	2 *pounds salmon steaks*
1 *celery stalk*	*gelatin*
parsley roots	

Prepare a court bouillon of fish trimmings (sole for example), one carrot, half an onion, one celery stalk, parlsey roots and a combination of half water and half dry white wine. When the bouillon is boiling, pour into another pot taking out the solid ingredients and simmer for fifteen minutes. Poach the salmon steaks in the bouillon for ten minutes. Set them on a cloth to cool, then pour some very thick jelly over them and chill. Garnish the salmon with lettuce, tomatoes, lemon, hard-boiled eggs and parsley. Serve with Sauce Vincent in a sauceboat. Serves four.

SUPRÊME DE SAUMON À L'OSEILLE

Sauce

1 *cup dry white wine*	*sorrel chiffonnade*
1/2 *cup Noilly Prat*	*lemon*
1 *cup fish stock*	
1/2 *pint 35% cream*	

To make the sauce, reduce one cup of dry white wine, half a cup of Noilly Prat and one cup of fish stock to about five or six tablespoons. Add the cream and heat over medium heat to obtain a sauce with a butter-like consistency. It is preferable to use a double-boiler or a *bain-marie*. To complete the sauce, make and add a sorrel chiffonnade (a mixture of lettuce and sorrel chopped and simmered in butter), rectify the seasoning and add a very light stream of lemon. For this stage of cooking, you should use an enamelled cast iron sauté pan, if possible. The result should be a sauce that coats a spoon fairly heavily. If the colour is dull, add an egg yolk to it.

Main Ingredients

1 *whole salmon*	*clarified butter*
salt and pepper	*white butter*

The salmon has to be sliced in filets (escalope) and the skin and bones removed. To do this, place the knife horizontally over the bones and cut horizontally following the spinal column to the tail. Turn the salmon over and make another incision from the tail to the head between the filet and the skin. Slice the meat into filets. Set these suprêmes, thinly sliced, into a saucepan that has been well buttered for the oven. Season with salt and pepper and brush the filets with clarified butter. Cook in the oven at a very high temperature, sprinkling re-peatedly with butter. The fish is done when you can look between the fibres of the flesh to see that it is just a bit raw. Beyond this stage the salmon becomes dry. Put the sauce on a shallow dish and set the suprêmes down without coating them with sauce. You might want to use a *fleuron* (a small, flaky pastry) as a garnish.

GIGOTIN D'AGNEAU AU PISTOU

Pistou

4 ounces pork (back) fat, finely chopped	1-1/2 tablespoons fresh basil
3 cloves garlic	1-1/2 tablespoons fresh parsley
	3 tablespoons breadcrumbs

Mix the ingredients and form an oblong lump. This is used to replace the quasi-bone from the leg of lamb.

Main Ingredients

    the pistou
    clarified butter
    1 small leg (gigot) of lamb with lots of flesh
    flaky pastry dough and a glaze made with an egg yolk diluted with water

Debone the leg of lamb and take out the quasi-bone; this should be done carefully without cutting the entire length of the meat. Fill up the cavity with the pistou. Reclose the leg with two or three small stitches. Roast the lamb in a preheated 500° F (260° C) oven for fifteen to twenty minutes. Turn the meat and sprinkle with clarified butter after eight to ten minutes. Roll out the pastry dough and cover the lamb with it, leaving the "handle" exposed. Seal the dough with water. Brush the surface of the dough with the glaze. To cook the pastry, put the lamb back in the oven for twenty minutes at 400° F (204° C). Serve with grilled tomatoes and potatoes à la parisienne sprinkled with chopped, fresh parsley.

Nicholas Francisco
Chef, Hampshire House, Boston

MUSSELS MARINIERE

1 gallon of mussels, still in their shells
  dry white wine
2 tablespoons fresh, chopped parsley
1 sprig fresh thyme
1 pinch fresh oregano (optional)
1 tablespoon chopped shallots
1/2 teaspoon pepper

1/2 cup heavy cream
1/4 pound butter

Put about 1/4 inch of white wine into a large covered kettle. Add the mussels, shallots, parsley, thyme, oregano and pepper. Cover the kettle and steam for about five minutes or until the shells open (any that fail to open should be discarded). Add the cream. Melt the butter in the broth or accompany the broth with melted butter. Serve on coquille shells with the broth. Serves four to six.

NOTE ON CLEANING MUSSELS Scrape off the barnacles, then clean the shells with a stiff brush under running water. Trim off the beard (this is easily done with scissors). Now they are ready to cook.

SCALLOPS ITALIENNE

3 pounds scallops
3/4 pound sliced mushrooms
2 sprigs fresh thyme
1 tablespoon chopped shallots
1 cup cooking sherry
2 tablespoons chopped, fresh parsley

2 cloves chopped garlic
1/2 cup heavy cream

Sauté the shallots and garlic in butter until limp. Add scallops and mushrooms. Cook over low heat for three minutes. Pour in the sherry, stirring well as you pour. Then add the fresh thyme and parsley. Pour in the cream and let the mixture cook until the sauce is creamy. Correct the seasoning with salt and pepper to taste. *Don't overcook the scallops, and don't boil the sauce, just simmer.* Excellent with rice pilaf. Serves five to eight.

Bernd Gabel
Executive Chef, Harbour Castle, Toronto

LES CUISSES DE GRENOUILLES

8 frogs' legs
1/4 teaspoon salt
1 dash pepper
1 dash aromate
3 ounces butter
1/2 teaspoon chopped shallots
8 teaspoons white wine
1/8 cup breadcrumbs (no crust included)

3-1/2 teaspoons white vermouth
8 teaspoons fish stock
1/2 lemon
1/2 cup 35% cream
1 tablespoon fresh, chopped chive
1 teaspoon peeled, pulped tomato

These are the ingredients for one serving. Multiply them by the number of portions you want. Season the frogs' legs with salt, pepper, aromate and lemon juice. Melt the butter, brush the frogs' legs on one side only and roll that side in the breadcrumbs. Put half the white wine and the fish stock into a deep frying pan and add the frogs' legs, breaded side up. Cook in the oven for ten minutes at a high temperature. Reduce the remainder of the white wine, shallots, fish stock, vermouth and tomato. Add the cream, bring to a boil and reduce by half. Strain and mix with the rest of the butter. Pour the sauce on a platter, sprinkle with fresh chive and put the frogs' legs on top.

ESCARGOTS CHATEAUNEUF

6 snails
2 ounces butter
1/2 teaspoon chopped shallots
1 teaspoon fresh, chopped tarragon
1/2 teaspoon freshly ground black pepper
8 ounces truffles, peeled and chopped
1/2 teaspoon fresh, chopped parsley

10 teaspoons white wine
3-1/2 teaspoons Pernod
7 teaspoons 35% cream
salt and garlic to taste

These are the ingredients for one serving. Multiply them by the number of portions you want. Sauté the shallots in butter. Add the tarragon, garlic and white wine. Reduce the liquid by half. Add the cream and Pernod and reduce by half again. Heat the snails in the sauce. Serve in a round dish, sprinkled with truffles and chopped parsley.

HUÎTRES PÊCHEUR

Americaine Sauce

1/3 cup butter	3/4 teaspoon pepper
3/4 cup flour	2 teaspoons aromate
6 cups fish stock	3/4 teaspoon Worcestershire sauce
2 tablespoons oil	
4 1/2 teaspoons tomato paste	
1/2 teaspoon fresh chopped tarragon	
4 1/2 teaspoons brandy	
4 1/2 teaspoons salt	

Melt the butter and stir in the flour to make a roue. Slowly stir in the fish stock. Simmer until the sauce thickens. Combine the remaining ingredients and add to the sauce. Simmer for five or ten minutes.

Main Ingredients

6 oysters (shells apart)	cayenne pepper to taste
1/2 teaspoon chopped shallots	salt to taste
1 teaspoon fresh, chopped oregano	1 egg yolk
1 ounce baby shrimp	1 ounce 35% cream, whipped
1 teaspoon butter	
2 ounces red vermouth	
4 ounces Amèricaine Sauce	

These are the ingredients for one serving. Sauté the shallots, baby shrimp and oregano in the butter. Deglaze with one ounce of vermouth. Reduce the liquid by half, pour in the Amèricaine Sauce and simmer for five minutes. Poach the oysters in the remaining half of the vermouth. Heat the oyster shells in the oven, then place the poached oysters in the shells. Add the leftover vermouth to the reduced sauce, add the egg yolk and fold in the whipped cream. Brush the oysters with the Sauce Pêcheur you have made and serve.

Arno Schmidt

Executive Chef, Waldorf-Astoria, New York

BEEF TIDBITS WITH SAVORY BEANS

1 pound beef sirloin or tenderloin tidbits cut in slivers one inch by
   one quarter inch
2 tablespoons oil
1-1/2 cups whole stringbeans
2 teaspoons butter
1 teaspoon chopped, fresh savory
   salt and pepper to taste

Heat the oil in a skillet. Rapidly sauté the meat over a hot flame until
lightly cooked on all sides. With a slotted spoon, remove the meat to a
serving dish. Cook the stringbeans for three minutes in rapidly boiling
water and drain. Put the butter in the meat skillet, add the savory and
season to taste. Toss the beans in the butter and herb mixture. Serve the
beans sprinkled over the beef. Serves four.

BROILED CHICKEN WITH BASIL

2 whole chickens (2-1/2 pounds each, split from the back)
   fresh basil leaves
2 tablespoons oil
1 tablespoon chopped, fresh basil leaves
4 tablespoons butter
1/2 a lemon
   salt and pepper

Push basil leaves under the chicken skin wherever possible. Season the
chickens with salt and pepper and rub with oil. Broil, skin up, in a very
hot oven for twenty minutes or until the skin is crisp and the chickens
are done. (Note: in gas ovens the chicken can be placed under the
broiler until light brown and then finished in the oven. In an electric
oven broiler, the process can be done in one step). Combine the butter,
basil, lemon juice, salt and pepper. Cut the chickens in attractive
pieces and serve with basil butter. Serves four.

PORK TENDERLOIN WITH SAGE AND APPLE

2 pork tenderloins (14-18 ounces each)
1 tablespoon oil
2 large Delicious apples
2 tablespoons butter
1 teaspoon coarsely chopped, fresh sage
  salt and pepper to taste

Rub the meat with the oil and some of the chopped sage. Season with salt and pepper. Roast in a 325° F (163°C) oven for forty-five minutes. Peel the apples, core and slice thinly. Remove the meat from the pan and pour off most of the fat. Add the butter to this pan and place it on the stove. Add the apples and cook quickly for four minutes. Sprinkle on the rest of the sage. Slice the meat and serve it on a bed of cooked apples. Serves four.

TOMATO AND MELON SALAD WITH BASIL

fresh tomatoes
melon (cantaloupe or honeydew)
fresh basil leaves
lemon juice
oil
salt and pepper

Arrange wedges of peeled fresh tomatoes and wedges of melon in an attractive pattern. Garnish with basil leaves. At the moment the salad is served, sprinkle to taste with lemon juice, oil, freshly ground pepper and salt.

Lluis Caner
Executive Chef, The New Orleans Hilton

WINSTON'S SALAD
---

3 heads, Bibb lettuce
3 medium size green peppers
2 medium size onions
1 cup white cheese
1/2 cup salad oil
1/3 cup wine vinegar
1 tablespoon Dijon mustard
1 tablespoon chopped, fresh chive
1 tablespoon chopped, fresh sorrel
1 tablespoon chopped, fresh tarragon

salt and pepper to taste

To make the dressing, place the cheese, salad oil, vinegar and mustard in a blender. Blend well and then add the seasoning and herbs. Let the dressing set in the refrigerator for five hours before serving.

To make the salad, clean the lettuce of all dark green leaves, wash well, cut in half and place on a serving platter. Top the lettuce with julienne strips of green pepper and onions, which have been precooked whole in a 375° oven, cooled and peeled. Serve the dressing in a sauceboat or gooseneck. Serves six.

ARTICHOKE BOTTOMS SAUTÉED WITH HERBS
---

12 artichokes, medium size
2 lemons, juiced
6 ounces unsalted butter
1 teaspoon chopped, fresh parsley
1 teaspoon chopped, fresh chervil
1 teaspoon chopped, fresh tarragon
1 teaspoon chopped, fresh chive

salt and pepper to taste

Peel the raw artichokes of all leaves to obtain the bottoms. Slice the bottoms julienne thin. Pour or squeeze the lemon juice over them. Sauté slowly until tender, add the herbs, stir and serve.

LLUIS' VEAL SCALOPE WITH CRAWFISH

Stuffing

> 4 ounces butter
> 9 ounces crawfish tails
> 1 cup fresh snow peas, sliced julienne thin
> 1/3 teaspoon chopped garlic
> 1/3 teaspoon chopped shallots
> 2 teaspoons chopped, fresh dill
> 1/2 teaspoon chopped, fresh basil
> 1/2 cup white Chablis
> 1/2 cup fish stock
>   salt, cayenne pepper to taste
> 1 pinch sugar
> 1 cup breadcrumbs

To make the stuffing, melt the butter in a sauté pan and sauté the crawfish tails lightly. Add the snow peas, garlic and shallots. Sauté for a few minutes longer, then add the herbs. Mix well, add the wine and reduce by half, then add the fish stock and season. Remove from the heat, add the breadcrumbs and stir well.

Main Ingredients

> 12 medallions of veal from the loin, 2-1/2 ounces each
> 1 cup flour
> 4 ounces butter
> 6 ounces crawfish tails
> 1/3 teaspoon shallots
> 1 teaspoon chopped, fresh dill
> 1/2 cup white Chablis
> 1/3 cup demi glacé
> 1/2 cup heavy cream
>   salt and pepper to taste

Flatten the veal medallions until they are very thin. Spoon the crawfish stuffing into the centre of six of them and cover with the remaining six, forming nice scallops. Season lightly, pass through the flour, sauté with butter and arrange on a serving platter. Sauté the 6 ounces of crawfish tails in the same pan, add the shallots, dill and Chablis, then add the *demi glacé* and heavy cream. Pour the mixture over the veal and serve. Serves six.

City Green

SAUCE VINAIGRETTE

---

6 tablespoons of olive or salad oil   1 pinch of salt (to taste)
1/4 teaspoon or more of dry mustard
1 tablespoon chopped, fresh green onions
1 very large pinch of chopped, fresh basil or tarragon leaves
2-3 tablespoons of wine vinegar or lemon juice
1 large pinch of freshly ground black pepper

Shake the ingredients in a small, sealed container and put in the refrigerator for about fifteen minutes. Just before pouring it over your fresh salad, shake again; toss well.

TARTAR SAUCE

---

2 tablespoons finely chopped, fresh parsley
1 tablespoon finely chopped, fresh chive
1 tablespoon finely chopped, fresh tarragon
1 tablespoon finely chopped, fresh chervil (optional)
1 cup mayonnaise
1 teaspoon finely chopped onion (optional)
1 tablespoon finely chopped capers
1 small sour pickle, finely chopped

Combine all the ingredients and blend well. If desired, add a little finely minced garlic. Yields about 1-1/4 cups.

HYDROPONIC HERB MAYONNAISE

1-1/2 tablespoons fresh tarragon leaves   1/2 teaspoon dry mustard
1 tablespoon chopped, fresh chive   1/2 teaspoon salt
1-1/2 teaspoons chopped, fresh dill   1/2 teaspoon sugar
1-1/2 teaspoons fresh marjoram   1 cup olive oil
1 tablespoon lemon juice   1-1/2 teaspoons vinegar
1 egg
6 raw spinach leaves, well washed, patted dry and coarsely chopped

Combine the spinach, herbs, lemon juice, egg and other seasonings in an electric blender jar. Blend at high speed for ten seconds. Immediately reduce the speed to low and add half the olive oil in a thin, steady stream. Stop the motor and add the vinegar. Blend at high speed and immediately add the remaining oil in a steady stream. The mayonnaise should form at once. Yields about 1-1/2 cups.

GREEN SAUCE

In Europe, where higher food prices and lower incomes are the norm, "la sauce c'est tout", and it often has to carry the day. Served ice-cold with boiled beef (cheaper cut) or fish, this renowned German sauce is delicious.

2 hard-boiled eggs   *2 tablespoons mustard*
1 pickle   *1/2 cup mayonnaise*
1 medium-size onion   *pepper and salt to taste*
1 clove garlic
1/2 lemon, juice and skin only (use a potato peeler to obtain the skin)
2 handfuls of a combination of most or all of these fresh herbs: chervil, sage, tarragon, chive, lovage, pimpernel (salad burnet), sorrel, borage, parsley, basil

The sauce is easier to make if you have a blender. You can replace the mayonnaise with one raw egg and one-half cup of oil. If not, chop the herbs (very fine), and the eggs, pickle and onion. Grate the garlic and lemon peel. Mix all the ingredients and season to taste. Refrigerate before serving. The flavours of the seasonings are reduced when the sauce is served very cold, so you should overdo it a bit with the salt and pepper. Yields two to three cups.

HYDROPONIC HERB CHEESE

This recipe is designed to outdo the tasty but expensive small herb cheeses imported from France, and at a fraction of the cost.

2 ounces blue or Roquefort cheese   *1/2 pound butter, melted*
1 pound dry cottage cheese   *1 sliver of onion*
1/2 pound sour cream   *1 clove garlic, chopped*
A mixture of these fresh herbs: parsley, chive, leaf of celery, lovage, chervil, basil, thyme, marjoram, savory. (The amount depends on your taste. Use leaves only.)

Put the cheese and sour cream into a blender jar. Add melted butter.
Cover the jar and turn the blender on low. Stop the motor frequently
and push everything down to get an even mixture. When these
ingredients are circulating well, add garlic, onion and salt to taste.
Now add the fresh herbs and taste frequently until desired flavour is
reached. (It helps to have one of your favourite French herb cheeses
nearby for comparison.) Pour the mixture into a bowl, cover and
refrigerate. The mixture will be liquid in the blender, but it will set in
the refrigerator.

HERB BASE FOR SOUPS AND SAUCES

Prepared in bulk in advance, this seasoned concentrate of fresh hydroponic herbs keeps for months in the freezer at the consistency of ice
cream. To use, simply take a few scoops from the container, fry them
briefly, then quench with water, milk or beef stock to release the
tantalizing herb flavours and fragrances.

> 4 handfuls of a mixture of fresh parsley, celery and lovage leaves,
>   combined in proportions of four to two to one
> 1/2 carrot, coarsely chopped
> 2 roots of turnip-rooted
>   (Hamburg) parsley
> 1/2 celeriac (European celery) root
> 1/2 cup oil
>   salt to taste
> 1 handful fresh chive (optional)
> 1 sliver onion (optional)
> 1/2 teaspoon garlic powder (optional)
> 1 tablespoon soy sauce (optional)
> 2 sprigs fresh chervil (optional)

Wash the herbs, parsley root and carrot. Peel the celeriac. Tear the herb
leaves and chop the stems so they won't jam the blender blades. Cut the root
vegetables into chunks. Drop everything into a blender jar, add oil, turn the
motor on at low speed. Slowly add just enough hot water to get the mixture
circulating well. Stop the motor intermittently and push everything down.
Add salt until the mixture is too salty to eat by itself. Wash a pickle jar and its
lid with hot water and use it to store the Herb Base in the freezer. This is a
delicious base for soups, sauces and even gravies; yields about one pint.

CHAPTER 10

Pollination

Most flowering types of vegetables require some kind of pollination by you when they are grown indoors, unless you plan to keep bees or other insects in your home. Often, pollination can be carried out by a gentle breeze or a simple shake of the stem. Beans, eggplants, peas, peppers and tomatoes are all capable of pollinating themselves in this manner, because the flowers contain both male and female parts (called hermaphroditic). A more certain method is to apply a small hand vibrator or an electric toothbrush to the stem. If you don't see pollen falling from the flower in a little cloud of dust, you could try using a small, inexpensive artist's brush. A Q-tip is often suggested, but I prefer the more gentle brush. In either case, gently swab the base of the staminal cone (see Figure 21) and you have accomplished your task.

Special attention must be given to vine-type vegetables such as cucumber, zucchini and cantaloupe, because these plants have both male and female flowers. Cross-pollination is necessary with these plants. The male and female flowers are easy to identify. The male flower is supported from its branch by a tiny, ordinary straight stem. The female flower, on the other hand, is supported by a stem shaped like the fruit that will eventually grow. In fact, this actually is the fruit or vegetable that will form once cross-pollination is carried out. To cross-pollinate, use your small brush again. Disturb the pollen in the male flower, carry it over to the female flower and disturb the pollen again.

It is good practice to repeat pollination and cross-pollination procedures for about three days to make sure you have been successful. Although wind and insects usually do the job outside, it is worthwhile to give nature a helping hand by using the same methods. One caution should be mentioned. Too high or too low a humidity can make it difficult to fertilize your flowers and can cause them to wither and die. Nevertheless, flowers do like rather high humidity for pollination and it seems that a good time for this is between about 10 AM and 2 PM. On the days you must pollinate, if the humidity level is considerably lower than desired, try misting the plants two or three times from early morning until noon. This will increase the humidity.

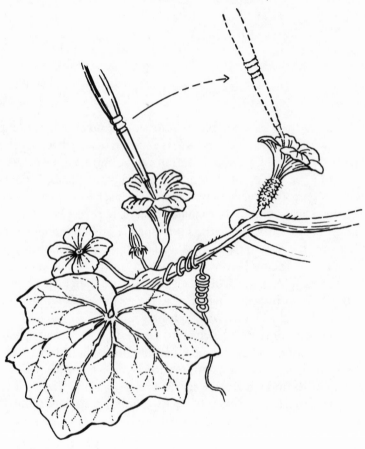

Figure 20. Pollinating a cucumber plant.

These simple steps are all there is to practical pollination and cross-pollination. Of course, on a more scientific level this can be a complex art, but here I am primarily concerned with effective procedures that will produce results. The bibliography lists several books and magazines where you can find a great deal more information on this subject.*

---

* One of the best explanations I have seen of pollination is Jennifer Bennett's "No Bees, No Breeze Gardening" that appeared in *Harrowsmith*, Issue 16, pages 79-85.

Figure 21. Pollinating a tomato plant.

CHAPTER 11

Outdoor
Hydroponics

Few books on hydroponics deal with the idea of moving a soilless garden outside. To my way of thinking, though, the whole point of hydroponics is to get the best possible year-round results. There is a great temptation for the home grower to lean back and say, "Outdoor gardening? Who needs it? I'm going to keep my garden in the basement all year. No wind, no bugs, no problems." It really isn't necessary to move your garden outdoors in summer, but if you don't, you'll be missing the opportunity to grow plants of tremendous proportions and yield. It is possible, for example, to root ten to twelve staking tomato vines in a single sixteen by twenty-four inch planter outdoors, spread them on a six foot wide trellis and let them grow to heights of seven to nine feet. There is ample nutrient in the planter for all and ample light from the sun. This is how to get yields of ten to twenty pounds per plant from each crop, much higher than indoors. If you are truly interested in results, it seems foolish to me not to go outdoors in summer.

Moving your garden outdoors takes planning, however, because you have to make your unit portable, and you have to know when the first frost-free day in your area is likely to be. When building or buying a hydroponic garden, it is a good idea to be on the lookout for such things as tea caddies with wheels or a small wheelbarrow. These can make transportation much easier.

The first frost-free day is a red letter one for soil gardeners. It's the date when all chance of (overnight) ground frost has passed. In the northern United States and most of Canada's southern belt, this is May 24th. The local Agricultural Office publishes this information for specific geographical areas. With a portable hydroponic unit, your outdoor growing season can start three to four weeks earlier than this date, because you have no ground frost to worry about. On a protected porch or balcony, you can take advantage of the heat given off by the building. However, if you simply take your plants outside in April or May and leave them there, you will probably kill them. Plants need to be "hardened off." That is, they have to become gradually accustomed to the cooler temperatures and higher light levels of an outdoor environment. This is done by moving them out for an hour or two during the warmest part of the day and increasing the time an hour or two every few days until they are able to withstand twenty-four hours a day outside. The entire hardening off process should take about a week or two.

For the first, early month of outdoor hydroponic gardening, it is still a good idea to listen closely to weather reports. When a freak frost is announced, cover your plants and planters with paper or plastic overnight. When the overnight low is announced as 32°F (0°C), it will still be about 37°F (+3°C) in your protected location. A low of 26°F (−3°C) means it's a good idea to move your plants back indoors for the night. In any case, be sure to set your plants in a protected spot with a southern or western exposure if possible.

Two months before the first frost-free day plant your seeds indoors under lights. Big plants are particularly suited for outdoor hydroponics, especially types that grow too tall or range too far for efficient indoor lighting. Staking tomatoes, pole beans, green peppers and cucumbers all do exceptionally well. If you are buying seedlings from a commercial grower rather than raising your own, select only the best. They should be dark green, medium tall and heavy stemmed. (Don't forget to remove all of the soil from the roots of any plants you purchase.) Leggy plants, either bought or raised, should be planted as deeply as possible, up to the first or second set of true leaves. Newly planted seedlings should be protected from direct sunlight for the first few days, so they don't get burned. Plant sunburn appears as whitish, leached-out leaves.

If you time the seeding and moving of your unit correctly you should have red, ripe tomatoes in June, long before soil gardeners, and lettuce, beans and peas even earlier. If you don't want to cut it quite that fine, allow an extra week or two after the first frost-free day.

What to Plant Outdoors

Tomatoes are the prime choice for outdoor hydroponics. They recapture the flavour long gone from supermarket produce, and the theoretical maximum yield is very high, twenty pounds per vine. In your first season, though, you're doing fine if you get about half that much. A fast growing, medium-sized staking variety produces more and better quality fruit than the larger hybrids. Tomatoes are grown quite close together in hydroponics, four to six inches. A good arrangement in a sixteen by twenty-four inch unit would be to set a row of five plants along the rear edge and fan them out against a wall on strings or trellises.

Staking tomatoes have to be pruned. This makes it easier to tie the vines and keep the plants in manageable shape. There are three ways of pruning: single-stem, double-stem or multiple-stem. Double- or multiple-stem pruning is the best in my experience. Let the first two or three suckers grow and pinch off only those above them. Permit the lower suckers to develop into a second, third or even fourth stem. All subsequent suckers should be removed from these stems. When pruning, especially in warm weather, my suggestion is to remove a branch from a plant each day or two. Excessive pruning at one time could cause

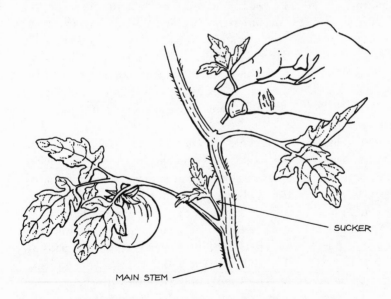

SUCKER

MAIN STEM

Figure 22. Prune tomatoes by pinching off the suckers that appear in the crooks between branches and the main stem of the plant.

shock. After the first fruit-set, remove the lower branches one or two at a time. After the next fruit-set, remove the branches between the first and second fruit-set the same way. Use pruning scissors if possible. It is also a good idea to do this indoors with your bush tomatoes. It keeps the energy going to the fruit rather than to the lower leaves, which by this time serve no useful function.

Intercropping and outcropping were described in Chapter 7, and the outdoor season is the time to take full advantage of your hydroponic growing area. In the planter where you have placed your five tomato vines, don't forget to plant pole beans in a corner. They will frame your garden with cheerful foliage while taking up little room in your planter. The remainder of the space is still available for a wide range of herbs and flowers. Be sure to pay attention to the rules for Companion Planting given in Chapter 7. In colder, more northern regions, try to get a good head start on the painfully short growing season.

Towards the end of autumn, it's time to move your garden back indoors. Because every latitude and location is different, find out from the local Agricultural Department when the first frost is expected. You will still have an extra month for growing at the end of the season over your dirt gardening friends, because of the protection and heat loss from your building and because your planters do not sit in or on the ground.

Before you move your garden indoors (and whenever you harvest a complete plant) remove the root stock from the growing medium. Also, check your plants and planters carefully to make sure that any insect infestations aren't taken indoors. Otherwise, there are no special instructions for taking your garden back inside. The plants you wish to keep will survive quite well, and there is little danger of temperature or light shock.

If you do find that insects are present, however, you must either terminate your plants, clean out your system and sterilize the growing medium, or spend a couple of weeks making sure you have eliminated all infestation, broken the egg hatching cycle and destroyed any eggs lying dormant in your gravel. Only after this is done is it safe to bring your units indoors. To sterilize the growing medium, place it into a foil roasting pan. Bury a potato in the centre of each pan. Set the pans in the oven at 450°F (232°C), and when the potato is done, your growing medium will be sterilized. The same should be done with the drainage medium, if you are using one, or you may wish to replace it completely. This would be a good time to add dolmitic lime (see Chapter 4), if you have found it necessary in the past.

Reminders for Outdoor Hydroponics

1. Move your garden outside gradually.
2. Early in the season check your newspaper for frost warnings and either cover your plants or move them indoors for the night.
3. Start your seedlings indoors under lights two months before you begin your move.
4. For the first few days, protect your seedlings from direct sunlight.
5. Take advantage of building heat loss and protection and put your plants against a wall. A south or west exposure is best.
6. Tie tall and climbing plants to stakes, strings or trellises.
7. Keep any air pumps out of the rain by simply using a longer air hose than you would indoors.
8. Before moving back indoors, check for insects.

CHAPTER 12

Helpful
Hints

I am firmly convinced that placing a chair beside your system every so
often and sitting there to get the feel of your plants is advantageous.
Plants give off many visual messages. It is up to you to learn how to
interpret those messages. You can do it by studying the appearance of
your plants and becoming totally familiar with each kind. When left to
itself, nature does a haphazard growing job. It is essential that you do
not leave everything up to nature after you have seeded your soilless
garden. Ten or fifteen minutes care a day, or at worst an hour a week,
will pay huge dividends in your crops.

Cleaning Your System

Cleanliness is a must around, as well as in the system. Remove dead
leaves before they rot, for this is an ideal place for fungus infection.
Keep a close watch for red spider and white fly infestations. They are the
two greatest insect problems in hydroponics. Insecticides will be discussed in detail later in the next chapter, but if you do use one, make sure it
isn't the same brand all the time. Insects build up a resistance to one
kind of insecticide very quickly. Also, try a little preventative spraying.

Once a year, or after every crop, clean out your system and sterilize
the growing medium. This can be done by picking out the worst of the
bits and pieces of roots and then placing the medium in the oven for

about an hour at 450-500°F (232-260°C). Your system should be flushed every thirty days to remove accumulated mineral hardness left by water additions. Accumulated minerals and salts will slow down your plants' growth. Flushing is done with plain water. If your system has drain holes, plug them temporarily and fill the planter to the brim. Don't worry about the plants. Let the water stand for about an hour and then drain away. If you are flushing the system because of a nutrient oversupply, operate the planter on plain water for a week and only then begin a nutrient solution again. Otherwise, you should return to a nutrient solution right away.

Keeping a Log

Although this book is directed at the novice, and scientific details have been kept at minimum, one scientific procedure is worthwhile. Keep a log of everything you do from day to day for each planter you have. Record the pH when checked, list the nutrient solution added, the amount of light, when seeded, when transplanted, first fruit, first harvest and the amount of harvest. Anything that can add to your knowledge later is worth putting into your log. This is especially true when you encounter problems along the way. Your log will provide background information that is useful in finding solutions. At the front of your log write up the check list that follows:

THE HYDROPONIC SYSTEM

1. Is there excessive water in the aggregate?
2. Is the aggregate too dry?
3. Is the system being drained too rapidly, too slowly?
4. Are pumping periods frequent and long enough?
5. Is the nutrient reservoir too low to pump?

WATER

1. What is the analysis of the water supply?
2. What is the pH level of the water; of the water and aggregate; of the water, aggregate and nutrient combined?

CLIMATE

1. Are the plants receiving sufficient light?
2. Are the plants receiving too much light?
3. Is there sufficient ventilation?
4. Is there a definite temperature difference between day and night?
5. Are the plants in a draft?
6. Is the air too dry or too humid?
7. Is the air clean and unpolluted by such things as a forced air heating system?
8. Is the area sterile or relatively clean?

It may even be a good idea to record the kinds of plants you have grown and the types of seeds you have used. (See sample log, page 131.)

Seeds

When considering which vegetable seeds to plant, for example, some attention should be given to hybrids. These seeds have been carefully controlled in cross-pollination to create a type that fills a particular void or ensures variety. In every instance of hybrid seeds, an explanation is given on the package or in a seed catalogue detailing why the hybrid was developed. Selection of seeds depends on the limits of your system and your requirements. Your requirements might be any of a dozen or so: self-pollinating, bush midget, staking, early fruiting and so on. In many instances, you will discover that, although a particular type of seed was not developed specifically for hydroponics, its qualities are such that it would appear to have been.

Growing midget seed varieties in particular can be an exciting and fun-filled part of hydroponic growing. Many of these are well suited to being grown indoors. There are three basic types: a small plant that produces normal fruit, a standard-sized plant that produces small fruit, and a small plant that produces small fruit.

Seed companies change the seeds they stock in retail outlets once a year, but many seeds are good for a long time. If you have part of a package left over from the previous year, it may not be necessary to throw it away and purchase a new one. Store leftover seeds in a dry, sealed container. To insure that they stay dry you might want to place a dessicant like silica or dried milk powder in the same container. The germination rate in hydroponics is very high, and you will usually lose only a few days checking out leftover seeds. The following list will give you some idea of how long commonly used seeds last:

Asparagus	3 years
Bean	3 years
Beet	4 years
Cabbage	4 years
Cantaloupe	5 years
Carrot	3 years
Cauliflower	4 years
Cucumber	4 years
Eggplant	4 years
Lettuce	5 years
Onion	2 years
Pea	3 years
Pepper	2 years
Radish	4 years
Spinach	3 years
Tomato	3 years

Pruning

When growing indoors, do not allow the top of the plant to get too far away from the root system. Almost every plant will grow larger in hydroponics than in soil, because the plants are getting a full measure of nutrients, air and water. *Bush* or *Tiny Tim* tomatoes are the only kinds you should grow indoors, and you should be sure to pinch off the tops when the plants reach a height of about 2-1/2 feet. Cucumbers, on the other hand, should be pinched off after seven sets of leaves. Pinching off in this way makes the plants more manageable under your lights and keeps the energy requirements close to the root system.

CHAPTER 13

Trouble Shooting

It has been repeated several times in this book that giving specific instructions or setting out rules is often difficult because of wide variations in such things as water quality, type of system, nutrient ingredients and environmental factors. The same is certainly true when we come to the subject of trouble shooting. What follows is an attempt to identify and deal with common problems encountered in home hydroponics. The fact that hydroponics depends to a large extent on grower experimentation can't be stressed often enough. This does not mean that the remedies given here don't work; they do, but because of variable factors you may encounter problems that are not covered in this or any other book, and it will be up to you to employ the knowledge you have gained to surmount them.

BLOSSOM DROP

Blossom drop can be an indirect result of transpiration stress where the plant is simply not able to supply enough energy to all its areas. Such problems will usually begin to show with the third set of blossoms, although if conditions are extreme it can occur with the first set. Sometimes, this malady can be corrected to some degree by giving the plant more phosphorus. Failure to achieve a satisfactory temperature differential between day and night will also cause blossom drop.

BLOSSOM SET

Indoor growing often creates problems with the blossoms on your vegetables. Nutrient, temperature, light and humidity all play a part. Nutrients were discussed in depth in Chapter 3. There must be a consistent temperature variance between day and night. If anything, vegetables like it cooler rather than warmer. Be sure to take advantage of all available indoor light and windows as well as using your growing lights. You may wish to add one to three incandescent bulbs to your lighting system, but be careful not to set them too close to the plants or you'll cook the blossoms. The effects of humidity on pollination have already been discussed. These problem areas should be carefully examined to prevent the flowers from dying and falling off before full cycle. Remember, hydroponics indoors is not natural. You are trying to recreate an outdoor environment, and you have to work at it.

BLACK SPOTS OR BLOSSOM END ROT ON TOMATOES

Although this is a somewhat involved topic, the basic reasons for black spots forming on the blossom side of your tomatoes are a transpiration stress on the vine or a calcium deficiency. Sometimes the two appear to be interdependent and sometimes they do not. The truth is that both circumstances are possible. When the deformity appears in the very small fruit, the problem could be mainly a calcium deficiency. On the other hand, when the rot attacks the older, larger fruit, the problem is more likely to be a lack of moisture.

What is happening here is that hydroponic plants usually grow more quickly and develop a smaller root system than those grown in soil. As the plant is growing, it uses a substance called calcium pectate which it manufactures to cement its cells together. If the plant is not getting enough calcium, the tomato will have dry cells and a black spot will form. The stress problem occurs because of the speed at which the plant grows plus a little outside help, such as extremely high temperatures or poor air circulation. This puts pressure on the root system to take in more water, which, because of its relatively small size, it is unable to do. The basic shortage at the time is calcium and/or water, but if you add more calcium to your nutrient, you will possibly upset its balance and cause other, indirect problems. Instead, you might try adding a little dolmitic lime. Besides, when you see the black spots forming it is already too late. The stress probably occurred about two weeks earlier. One of the symptoms is wilting of most of the leaves.

There is no cure for blossom end rot, only prevention. If you suspect a calcium deficiency, use a foliar spray. In hot weather, pour fresh water over your growing medium to saturate the roots and try to reduce extremely high temperatures. Increase air circulation.

BOLTING OF LETTUCE

Lettuce is a cool weather crop and will bolt if it is too warm or if it doesn't get enough light from germination to partial maturity. Give it all the light you can in the early stages. Grown outdoors, lettuce should be kept in a cool, shady place after partial maturity. It doesn't need full sunlight.

BOLTING OF RADISHES

Like lettuce, radishes need a lot of light at the start, and your luck will be better outdoors than indoors. However, this is no reason not to try it inside. I would suggest that when growing radishes you devote a whole planter to them, or at least a single planter for root vegetables, and use only water for the first three weeks. Until the seedlings are well developed, use only vermiculite and then put one-half inch of aggregate on the top to cut down on algae build-up.

DAMPING OFF

This disease is also called root rot, although damping off applies more to seeds and root rot to plants. This is a fungus disease caused by a variety of fungi. It strikes seeds, which will turn mildewy and fail to grow. This condition is probably due to the fact that the hydroponic watering system being used is excessive at a particular time for a particular variety of seed. Your planter could also be in a location that keeps it too damp, dark and cool. In plants, the roots turn brown and rot. One of the answers is an all-purpose fungicide. Be sure to follow the directions on the container.

DROOPING LEAVES

Check to see that your plants are getting enough water. Make sure that the pump of your automatic system is functioning properly. If these two things are in good order it is possible that your nutrient concentration is too high; the solution is too salty and your plants can't use it. Flush the system and run it on plain water for a week, then begin with the nutrient again. Keep in mind that the lack of water may have to do with transpiration problems caused by excessive temperatures in an area with poor air circulation. See Black Spots and Tomato Leaf Curl. Drooping leaves and leaf curl look alike to the novice.

INSECTS

Just about the only insects you'll have to contend with are red spider, aphids and white fly. Two good commercial insecticides are *Diazinone* and *Malathion*. *House and Garden Raid* is also good. They are safe to use and break down into harmless components within several days. For this reason, always mix a fresh batch and repeat the application every few days until the pests are gone. Some insecticides are dangerous to the skin, so follow directions carefully.

Try not to use insecticide on the edible parts of your plants. After using an insecticide, harvest no earlier than a week after the last application, and wash your crops well. Alternate your insecticides, since insects develop immunities rapidly. If you have soil-growing house plants within range of your planter that are infected with red spider, you will often find a transference to celery and cucumbers. Try to keep soil house plants separate from your hydroponic area.

The best cure is prevention. Remove all dead leaves from your plants and check those you purchase carefully. Keep your units clean.

Some insects, of course, are your plants' best friends. Bees and wasps pollinate the blossoms of your flowering vegetables, while ladybugs eat the eggs of insect pests. Other critters, however, are after the same thing you are — the crop.

No one really likes using insecticides. For those people who are concerned about the contents of many commercial kinds, one of the new organic insecticides might be preferable. These are powders based on diatomiseous earth that pierce and dehydrate the insect. They are harmless to man, animals and plants, and merit experimentation. The only drawback is the sometimes unsightly white powder all over the leaves. Organic solutions are also available. Here are two organic bug sprays you can make yourself.

All-Purpose Organic Spray

Chop three ounces of garlic cloves in a grinder or blender and soak for twenty-four hours in two tablespoons of mineral oil. Dissolve one-half ounce of oil-based soap in one pint of water and add to the garlic mixture. Stir well, strain and use in your hand sprayer.

Organic Hot Spray

Into a grinder or blender put one whole clove of garlic with skin, three large onions, plus one hot pepper, or two tablespoons of Tabasco sauce, or a level tablespoon of cayenne pepper. Barely cover the mixture with water and let it stand overnight. Next day mash it through a sieve. Then strain it through a paper towel or a Melitta coffee filter into a one gallon jug. Keep adding water over the residue in your towel or filter until the jug is full. Use in your hand sprayer.

LIMP LETTUCE

When they are grown in the sun, lettuce leaves are sometimes too limp to serve. They will crisp up nicely for your salad if you wash them in cold water, shake gently and put them in a plastic bag in the refrigerator for an hour before using.

MISSHAPEN OR DEFORMED TOMATOES

Two of the more common deformities are rough skins and misshapen fruit with skin that looks like a peeled orange. Both are usually caused by temperature factors. Failure to have a satisfactory day-night temperature variance can cause roughened fruit. Too low a night temperature and too low a day temperature can cause the same problem. There can be other reasons, but these are the most common for the home grower. The peeled orange syndrome is more likely to be caused by severe temperature fluctuations during a brief interval at blossom set. For information dealing strictly with tomatoes, see the Bibliography.

MIXING MEDIA

For those growers using both a growing and a drainage medium, it will soon become apparent that as you move plants in and out of your garden the two media get mixed up. There is no harm in this at all.

NUTRIENT FOR OUTDOORS

When growing outdoors, it sometimes happens that your plants will need less nutrient than they would indoors. Overfeeding causes drooping leaves and tip burn, and it will slow plant growth much more than underfeeding. The answer is to flush and start over again with a new nutrient solution.

OVERFEEDING

The most common mistake made by novices is that they may feel that more is better. The result is overfeeding. This burns the plants (see paragraph above). It is much safer to run the nutrient solution on the lean side. If the plants get too little nutrient, you will know they need more because the veins of their leaves will turn yellow or pale. Just add a pinch of nutrient and they'll turn green again almost overnight.

PATCHY GROWTH

Better growth in one area of a planter than another indicates that the nutrient solution is unevenly distributed. Simply pour your nutrient solution over the aggregate by hand. If this doesn't work, check your pump and lines.

RAIN OVERFLOW

In outdoor growing, a heavy rainfall may fill your planters to the brim. You should syphon off the excess water or have a drainage hole at the desired maximum level. Try to estimate the amount of water you have drained and make careful calculations of the correct amount of nutrient to add. A light rainfall will likely have an insignificant effect on the nutrient solution, so don't tamper with it.

SALT AND MINERAL BUILD-UP

White crystals forming on your growing medium indicate that flushing is necessary.

SPINDLY GROWTH

This condition is caused by insufficient light.

SUNBURN

White, bleached-looking areas appear on the leaves when planters are moved too quickly outdoors into bright sunlight. Keep the plants shaded for a few days or make the transition gradually to allow plant cells time to adapt to high light levels.

TIP BURN

The tips or margins of the leaves turn brown. The cause is overfeeding. Flush the system and start over.

TOMATO LEAF CURL

This problem is probably caused by excessive pruning in hot weather, or by an oppressively high indoor temperature. The latter could be a warning to look out for future blossom end rot. Leaf curl could also be an infection, but this is unlikely in hydroponics, because the fungi causing such infections live in soil. See Drooping Leaves.

WATER STRESS

See Black Spots.

WILTING

Periodic wilting of leaves is caused by a lack of moisture. This usually happens during the hottest part of the day. Immediately pour water over the surface of the aggregate. The best remedy is prevention, so you should probably do this every day at the hottest time.

YELLOW LEAVES

When a vegetable is nearing the end of its fruitful life, its older leaves will usually turn yellow and die. This is normal. In most other cases, yellowing older leaves means that the plants are getting too much water. Because of the porous aggregate, this is a rare occurrence in hydroponics. But if it does happen, reduce the water supply. The reduction method will depend on the type of system you have. For instance, you might keep your planter half full for awhile, shut your pump off from 11:00 PM to 7:00 AM for a continuous flow system, or eliminate a pumping period for a flood type.

When younger leaves yellow or when they turn a distinctly lighter green than older leaves, try adding a pinch of nutrient. Wait a few days and they'll turn green again. If not, add a little more.

Appendix: A Sample Log

SIMPLE pH TESTS

	Date and pH reading							
Water								
Water and nutrient								
Water and growing medium								
Water, nutrient and growing medium								
Water and phosphoric acid*								
Water, nutrient and phosphoric acid*								
Water, growing medium and phosphoric acid*								
Water, nutrient, growing medium and phosphoric acid*								

*Or neutralizer such as vinegar.

CHECK LIST

Function	Date / Observation											

System

Excessive moisture in aggregate												
Aggregate too dry												
Drainage too rapid												
Drainage too slow												
Frequency of pumping periods												
Depth of nutrient reservoir												

Water

Water analyses obtained												
pH tests carried out												

Climate

Sufficient light												
Too much light (i.e. heat)												
Ventilation												
Day/night temperature differential												
Drafts in room												
Humidity												
Clean air												
Cleanliness of area												

Note: see page 118 for information on keeping a log.

DAILY ACTIVITIES *

Date	Item

*For example: nutrient supplied, water added, phosphoric acid (neutralizer) added, pollination, flushing, temperatures, number of vegetables harvested and their approximate weight.

Bibliography

HYDROPONICS

Bridwell, Raymond. *Hydroponic Gardening.* Santa Barbara, Calif.: Woodbridge Press, 1974.

A large part of this book deals with greenhouses and commercial systems. Bridwell knows his subject and writes with an easy style, but one that occasionally lapses into a "talking down to you" manner.

Dickerman, Alexandra and John. *Discovering Hydroponic Gardening.* Santa Barbara, Calif.: Woodbridge Press, 1975.

This is a fun book that deals more with how the authors discovered hydroponics than the subject itself. It is interesting but not ideal for the person who seriously wants to learn about hydroponics.

Douglas, James S. *Advanced Guide to Hydroponics.* New York: Drake Publishers, 1976.

In this book, Douglas proves without doubt that he is one of the world masters of hydroponics. However, it is a rather weighty technical work and would prove valuable only to the person deciding to enter hydroponics on a commercial or semi-commercial scale.

Douglas, James S. *Beginners Guide to Hydroponics.* New York: Drake Publishers, 1973.

Here is a good introduction to hydroponics written by the man who many have come to feel is the father of modern hydroponics. Still, one-half of the book is given over to house plants and areas of little concern to the indoor vegetable grower.

Douglas, James S. *Hydroponics: The Bengal System.* New York: Oxford University Press, 1977.

You don't have to live in India to make full use of this book. It is most certainly ahead of its time. Douglas deals with many areas of concern and introduces the reader to the uses of hydroponics in space satellites, on the moon and back on earth for feeding people and livestock.

Ellis, Carleton, and Miller W. Swaney. *Soilless Growth of Plants.* New York: Reinhold Publishing Corporation, 1947.

Like Douglas, these authors are early pioneers and researchers of soilless growing. The book is interesting and worthwhile reading, and it covers a wide range of topics, including growing flowers in glass wool and plants in jars of water. The book first appeared in 1938, and like others of that era it details the vast number of hydroponics investigations then being tried; many of them are adaptable for the do-it-yourself enthusiast.

Harris, Dudley. *Hydroponics: Growing Without Soil.* Capetown: Purnell, 1974.
The author gives excellent attention to constructing soilless gardens and the general maintenance of your gardens. This is one of the early books, written by a knowledgeable person. It has had several printings.

Nicholls, Richard E. *Beginning Hydroponics.* Philadelphia: Running Press, 1977.
This is one of the best modern books for introducing the novice to the subject. While it lacks good follow-up information, the author writes in a clear, easy to understand fashion.

Resh, Howard M. *Hydroponic Food Production: A Definitive Guidebook for the Advanced Home Gardener and the Commercial Hydroponic Grower.* Santa Barbara, Calif.: Woodbridge Press, 1978.
Although recently published, the Resh book is a classic already. This is an exhaustive study that surely will become the textbook throughout North America if not the world. It is a must for the commercial grower.

Sherman, Charles E., and Hap Brenizer. *Hydro-Story.* Occidental, Calif.: Nolo Press, 1976.
This is a very interesting and attractive book with some superb drawings for home units, greenhouses and solar greenhouses. The book is presented in such an enjoyable manner that it makes an ideal general introduction to hydroponics.

INDOOR GARDENING UNDER LIGHTS

Cherry, Elaine C. *Fluorescent Light Gardening.* New York and Toronto: Van Nostrand Reinhold Ltd., 1965.
A very complete and easy to read book. The author's credentials are impeccable, and she answers all your questions about gardening under lights, including where to grow your plants, how to grow them and, most important, just what fluorescent lights are.

Kranz, Frederick H. and Jacqueline L. *Gardening Indoors Under Lights.* Markham, Ontario and New York: Penguin Books, 1976.
This books covers the theory and practice of balanced lighting and includes a chapter on salad greens.

HERBS

Lust, John. *The Herb Book.* New York: Bantam, 1974.
This is the most complete catalogue of "nature's miracle plants" ever published. Contents include herbs and history, getting and keeping plants, herb preparations and medicinal values. This book is a must for the herb enthusiast.

Previs, John. *Herb Growers Guide: Cooking, Spicing and Lore.* Philadelphia, Pa.: Running Press, 1974.

An ideal book for the enthusiast, it lists generic information, ancient herb uses, growing properties, modern uses and other general information.

Simmons, Adelma G. *Herbs to Grow Indoors, for Flavor, for Fragrance, for Fun.* New York: Hawthorne Books, 1969.

Simmons explains the qualities of each herb in such a lively manner that its fragrance almost leaps from the page. The complete chapter on herb recipes lives up to the subtitle.

GENERAL GARDENING

The books listed here have nothing to do with hydroponics, but they could prove invaluable to the novice, because any of them will provide information on the produce you plan to grow in your home unit.

McDonald, Elvin. *How to Grow Vegetables and Herbs from Seeds.* New York: Mason/Charter, 1977.

This book contains wonderful descriptions of one hundred and sixteen vegetables and herbs started from seeds, plus other general information. Comments, days to harvest, germination times, etc. are all included. Remember, though, that planting instructions will not be the same for hydroponics as they are for soil, so make allowances for being able to plant your seeds closer together.

Mulligan, Bill. *The Vegetable Gardener's Answer Book.* New York: Mason/Charter, 1977.

A lively, interesting book with lots of general gardening information presented to the reader by asking the same questions every other gardener asks and then providing the answers.

Philbrick, Helen and John. *The Bug Book: Harmless Insect Control.* Vermont: Garden Way Publishing, 1974.

Although hydroponic gardening does not usually include insect problems, some infestations and diseases can spread from soil to your soilless garden and from outdoor to indoor gardens. The Philbrick book is unique because it uses the "Bio-Dynamic" method of insect control, first established by Dr. Rudolf Steiner in 1924. This method, including prevention instructions, cannot effect the food chain.

Raymond, Dick. *Vegetable Gardening Know How.* Vermont: Garden Way Publishing, 1977.

This is a first-class book with a wealth of information presented in easy-to-read terms. It covers a very wide range of topics from pest control to plant diseases to planning a garden, as well as thirty-five pages of illustrated vegetable descriptions and storage information.

Riotte, Louise. *Success with Small Food Gardens.* Vermont: Garden Way
Publishing, 1977.
  Another superb book that deals with outdoor gardens, but one with a
great deal of information that can be adapted to hydroponics. Little known
fruit bearing shrubs, flower recipes, pruning and staking in small areas are all
included.

MAGAZINES

Harrowsmith — published monthly by Camden House Publishing Limited,
Camden East, Ontario, Canada K0K 1J0
  Without a doubt this is the finest North American publication for the
person who wants a more natural life style. Whether you are an urban dweller
looking for pure jam recipes or a country person wondering how to raise bees,
this attractive, professional magazine is fun, informative reading.

House Plants and Porch Gardens — published ten times a year by Scrambling
Press, Inc., Aldwyn Center, Villanova, Pa. 19085
  Although this magazine only occasionally prints articles on hydroponics,
it carries many superb pieces on most aspects of home gardening. Many of these
articles can be adapted by the hydroponics enthusiast.

The Mother Earth News — published bi-monthly from 105 Stoney Mountain
Rd., Hendersonville, North Carolina 28739
  This excellent magazine was one of the first in its field. It is published for
today's "turned-on" people, no matter what their age. Heavy emphasis is
placed on alternative life styles, ecology, working with nature and doing more
for less.

Natural Life — published by Natural Dynamics, Inc., P.O. Box 640, Jarvis,
Ontario, Canada N0A 1J0
  The subtitle, "Access to Self-Reliant Living," says it all. This is an
excellent magazine that carries wide ranging articles on such topics as herbs,
natural foods, organic gardening and alternate life styles.

GOVERNMENT PUBLICATIONS

Your local Agricultural Department probably has dozens of free publications
that will help you sort out problems and extend your knowledge in specific
areas. Three excellent ones in Canada are listed below.

Soilless Culture of Commercial Greenhouse Tomatoes. Publication 1460.
Agriculture Canada, revised 1978.

Tomato Colour Defects. Factsheet Order No. 75-003. Ministry of Agriculture
and Food, Ontario Government, January, 1975.

Tomato Disease. Publication 1479. Agriculture Canada, 1972.

Resource List

HYDROPONIC EQUIPMENT AND SUPPLIES

Aqua-Ponics 17221 East Seventeenth Street, Santa Anna, California 92701
Aqua-Ponics carries everything required by the home hydroponic enthusiast, including starter and backyard greenhouse kits, pH test kits, pumps, timers, nutrients, and mercury and halide lights.

City Green Hydroponics Corporation 598 Bell Road, Newark, New York 14513
This is a subsidiary of City Green Hydroponics Inc., Toronto (see below). Persons living in the United States should correspond with and order from the Newark address.

Eco Enterprises 2821 N.E. 55th Street, Seattle, Washington 98105
Eco Enterprises sells a complete line of kits, lighting (including metal halide), and build-your-own supplies.

Environmental Dynamics 12615 South La Cadena Drive, Colton, California 92324
This company carries greenhouse and greenhouse hydroponic kits, nutrient, starter kits and gravity feed systems.

City Green Hydroponics Inc. 1134 Yonge Street, Toronto, Ontario, Canada M4W 2L8
Manufacturers of City Green Hydroponic Systems, including starter, indoor and outdoor kits. Everything for the home builder is carried: pumps, pH test kits, phosphoric acid, light fixtures, fertilizer salts, trace elements, books, nutrient. Kits and materials may be ordered from Canada or the U.S.A. (see City Green Hydroponics Corporation above).

The Science Shop 137 Yonge Street, Toronto, Ontario, Canada M5C 1W6
This fine little shop sells a myriad of items of scientific interest. The home hydroponic grower can obtain pH test kits and solutions, as well as nitrates, phosphates and trace elements for mixing homemade nutrients.

Resh Greenhouses Ltd. 319-119 West Pender Street, Vancouver, B.C. V6B 1S5
The only company we know of in Canada that manufactures a greenhouse specifically for the northern environment.

NUTRIENTS (See also Hydroponic Equipment and Supplies)

Consolidated Laboratories Suite 118, 910 South Hohokam Drive, Tempe, Arizona 85281

This company makes a 7-7-19 nutrient with nine trace elements. It comes in either five or twenty-five pound packages. Although the quantity is high, the price is right.

Robert B. Peters Company   2833 Pennsylvania Street, Allentown, Pennsylvania 18104

This company has a 5-11-26 nutrient that is used in conjunction with calcium nitrate. Both are sold in twenty-five pound bags and would last a long time. However, the information provided by the company would allow you to mix several formulae from the two components.

ORGANIC NUTRIENTS

While the people involved in supplying organic nutrients appear to have little, if any, hydroponic experience, they do try to be most helpful. However, those wishing to use an "organic" nutrient as opposed to a "chemical" nutrient will find it virtually impossible to supply all the nutrient requirements for vegetables by purely "organic" means. My information is that some form of salts or nutrient supplement will be required. For example, the Laters Fish Fertilizer has an N-P-K rating of 5-1-1 which is far too low in phosphorus and potassium. If you do decide to use such nutrients, be prepared for some very powerful odors.

Eaton Valley Agricultural Services   C.P. 25, Sawyerville, Quebec, Canada J0B 3A0

This company carries Seacrop, a liquid seaweed concentrate, and fish emulsion.

Jenkins Hardware and Seeds   P.O. Box 2424, London, Ontario, Canada N6A 4G3

Blood meal and Laters Fish Fertilizer are available from this store.

Naturally Green   322 Lindley Place, Bozeman, Montana 59715

Many organic ingredients may be ordered from this address.

pH TEST KITS

The smaller and cheaper test kits are listed under Hydroponic Equipment and Supplies. The following companies are mentioned for those people interested in more accurate measurements.

Analytical Measurements   31 Willow Street, Chatham, New Jersey 07928
    or in Canada
2428 Islington Ave. N., Etobicoke, Ontario M9W 3X8

Their pH tester, Model 107, costs about $125 in the United States and about $145 in Canada.

Taylor Chemicals   7300 York Road, Baltimore, Maryland 21204

This company has a two slide combination tester that will give a very accurate reading in a satisfactory range. It sells for about $55 in the United States. The equipment is permanent, and the solution (easily replaced) will provide about ninety tests.

SEEDS

Alberta Nurseries and Seeds Limited Bowden, Alberta, Canada T0M 0K0
This company produces a fine colour catalogue with a special gourmet section, as well as sections on decorative shrubs, evergreens, standard seed varieties and garden aids. Also sells City Green supplies.

Burpee Seed Company Warminster, Pennsylvania 18991; Clinton, Iowa 52732; Riverside, California 92502
This is one of the largest seed companies.

Dominion Seed House Georgetown, Ontario, Canada L7G 4A2
Another fine catalogue, listing a wide variety of seeds.

Harris Seeds Moreton Farm, Rochester, New York 14624
A long established, conscientious company with a fine list.

Johnny's Selected Seeds Albion, Maine 04910
An outstanding seed list, with some very interesting varieties.

Ontario Seed Company P.O. Box 144, Waterloo, Ontario, Canada N2J 3Z9
This is a long established, reliable company that carries seeds and an excellent variety of gardening supplies. Also sells City Green supplies.

Otto Richter & Sons, Ltd. Goodwood, Ontario, Canada L0C 1A0
This company carries an outstanding collection of common and unusual herbs, many of which are grown on the premises. The illustrated catalogue costs 50c and is well worth the investment.

W. H. Perron & Co., Ltd. 515 Labelle Boulevard, Laval, Quebec, Canada H7V 2T3
Both seeds and gardening supplies are available. This is a large, well-established company. Also sells City Green supplies.

Redwood City Seed Co. P.O. Box 361, Redwood City, California 94064
Rare herb and spice seeds are available.

Stokes Seeds Ltd. P.O. Box 10, St. Catharines, Ontario, Canada L2R 6R6
or
P.O. Box 548 Buffalo, New York 14240
Stokes carries an especially fine stakeless tomato seed. Also sells City Green supplies.

Hydroponic Associations

There are probably numerous hydroponic associations in the world. Here are the addresses of three that you may want to join:

The Hydroponic Association of America,
P.O. Box 516,
Brentwood,
California   94513

International Working Group on Soilless Culture,
P.O. Box 52,
Waginen,
The Netherlands

For updated information and periodical bulletins, please contact the author,
Stewart Kenyon at this address:
1134 Yonge Street,
Toronto, Ontario.
M4W 2L8

Index